Markets and Authorities

In Memory of Susan Strange

Aylesbury, August 1998

Markets and Authorities

Global Finance and Human Choice

Edited by

Jochen Lorentzen

Associate Professor of International Business, Copenhagen Business School, Denmark

Marcello de Cecco

Professor of Monetary Economics, University of Rome, 'La Sapienza', Italy

Edward Elgar
Cheltenham UK, Northampton, MA, USA

Published by
Edward Elgar Publishing Limited
Glensanda House
Montpellier Parade
Cheltenham
Glos GL50 1UA
UK

Edward Elgar Publishing, Inc.
136 West Street
Suite 202
Northampton
Massachusetts 01060
USA

A catalogue record for this book is available from the British Library

Library of Congress Cataloging in Publication Data

Markets and authorities : global finance and human choice / edited by Jochen Lorentzen, Marcello de Cecco.
p.cm.
  Includes index.
    1. International finance. 2. Speculation.
    I. Lorentzen, Jochen. II. de Cecco, Marcello.
HG3881.M33345 2002
337–dc21
                                                      2002020238

ISBN: 1 84064 591 1

Printed and bound in Great Britain by MPG Books Ltd, Bodmin, Cornwall

Contents

Tables

Contributors

Pier Francesco Asso, University of Palermo, Italy

David Calleo, SAIS, Johns Hopkins University, USA

Marcello de Cecco, University of Rome, Italy

Ronald Dore, London School of Economics, UK

Charles P. Kindleberger, Massachusetts Institute of Technology, USA

Jochen Lorentzen, Copenhagen Business School, Denmark

Louis W. Pauly, University of Toronto, Canada

Preface

The idea for this book was conceived in a restaurant just outside Porta San Mamolo in Bologna in November 1998, barely a month after Susan Strange's death. The Asian crisis of the previous year and the unfolding rouble meltdown were the topics of discussion. David Calleo remarked how right Susan had been in predicting how and why these things would continue to happen. We decided to invite friends Susan had worked with during her time at the European University Institute (EUI) in Fiesole, to pick up the discussion of the problems of the global financial system where she had left it. *Dai suoi amici 'italiani'*, became the organising principle. The first step was to recruit Marcello de Cecco as co-editor. In May 1999 an editorial statement suggesting a focus for the present volume went out to quite a large group of people and met with an encouraging response. It was only then that we found out about another project in the making (Thomas C. Lawton, James N. Rosenau, and Amy C. Verdun (eds) (2000), *Strange Power: Shaping the Parameters of International Relations and International Political Economy*, Aldershot: Ashgate) among whose contributors were many students of Susan's. In her capacity as PhD advisor at EUI, Susan often referred to herself as 'midwife'. I belong to her flock, too; this is thus the second published instance of partial baby talk. In January 2000 Elgar agreed to publish the manuscript. The rest, as they say, is history. More precisely, since academics can get away with things not acceptable in most other professions, it is a history with roughly a one-year delay.

Most of the editing and my own writing took place in the summer of 2001 in Caselline, a village half an hour north of Florence not quite yet part of the Mugello. Susan and I were neighbours in that valley in 1992, before she left Italy for England and the EUI for the University of Warwick. It is a beautiful area and we used to go for hikes in the immediate surroundings and the Apennines. Ten years later, the lady who with a generous helping of punch followed by mountains of *tortelli di patate* nursed us back to life in front of her fireplace in a tiny hamlet close to the Giogo Pass after 5 hours of cold, torrential rains had completely drenched us, still remembers *la professoressa inglese* who at almost 70 was crazy enough to brave the elements instead of staying at home and keeping dry. Perhaps it was this physical toughness that helped Susan in her professional life defy conventional wisdom and take on pretty much anybody that wielded power with arrogance, or unwisely.

Outspoken commentators – especially those outside the mainstream – are often remembered for their rough edges. No-nonsense attitudes seldom go well with the etiquette that prevails in the corridors of power. But Susan wasn't just tough. She cared deeply about people. In 1997 I had a house guest from Sarajevo who overlapped with her. The young man had fought in the Bosnian army defending the city and subsequently completed a masters degree in international studies during which he came across some of Susan's works. To him, the sad and tragic story of the Balkan wars meant that he was a citizen of a failed society and had pretty much nothing to offer the world, let alone be good company for a famous academic. Susan took him out to dinner and quietly and patiently tried to convince him that the opposite was true: that the world depended on people like him to build something from the ruins and to ensure that things would never go so badly wrong again. This tenderness was as much part of her humanity as toughness accompanied her intellectual pursuits. Perhaps the combination of the two accounts for the impact she has had as an academic since the 1970s. She did not let go of these two traits after she learned that she had only a year left to live. On the tough side, she continued writing and, as ever, her essays did not beat around the bush. On the tender side, she continued to be there for her friends and tried hard to make her departure from this world easy on everybody. Susan's is a story of great human spirit.

Back to hiking. One weekend morning in early 1993 when she was visiting our valley from England we were clambering up a steep ascent. Susan was a little out of breath, not because she wasn't in shape but because she never stopped commenting on the many different flowers along our path. I asked her who her heroes were. She paused briefly and gave two names. Charles Kindleberger was one of them. I am very grateful to Professor Kindleberger for having graciously agreed to contribute to this volume, for his good humour, and for his timeliness. If he had been in charge of this project, the publication date would be 2001 (and we might already be in the second edition). The same is true for Francesco Asso who also helped me compile the index. David Calleo, Lou Pauly, and especially Ron Dore worked hard to make this book more than the sum of its individual contributions. My thanks go to all of them.

Global finance is so dynamic in part because it attracts great talent. The very least critical observers can do is to try to match the talent to probe why the global financial system, directly or indirectly, causes human suffering, and to consider alternative arrangements. This is what this book is about.

jl, Vejby (Denmark), April 2002

ix

Introduction

Jochen Lorentzen

Why *Markets and Authorities*? And why *Global Finance and Human Choice*? The short answer is that we are interested in what makes the global economy tick. Who, if anybody, runs the show? What is behind the nuts and bolts of the way the world economy affects our lives? And who benefits from the present state of affairs, and who suffers? The focus on global finance – as opposed to many other things global one might usefully discuss – results from the capacity of financial markets to wreck the orderly functioning of the capitalist system. Of course, all sorts of shocks can play havoc with how people try to make a living; with how firms try to make intelligent investment decisions; and with how public authorities try to create a general framework conducive to growth and prosperity. To name just a few, hurricanes, wars – whether real or commercial – endemic corruption, and diseases such as Aids or malaria all take their toll on economic activity. But most of these problems are geographically limited, and not all of them are under direct human influence. By contrast, when increasingly integrated financial markets spin out of control, the negative consequences are potentially felt all over the globe. And although financial crises are at times not manageable because policy intervention is up against something too big and too complex, the structure of financial markets is ultimately a question of human choice: what we get is what we – or at least some of us – want. That was the short answer to why this collection of essays bears this title. Now comes a longer explanation.

When people die who have made important contributions to human knowledge, it is customary to pay homage to their achievements. Susan Strange died in October 1998. She was our colleague, teacher, and friend. Under various circumstances and in different places, Susan helped us understand how the world works, and why. Like any author, she was always curious to see how her peers reacted to her work. As a fierce debater and provocative writer, she normally did not have to wait long for someone to take issue with her arguments. But regardless of whether reviewers agreed or disagreed with her, she was mainly interested in whether the ensuing discussion contributed to what we know about the world economy, and

1

perhaps to what we might suggest for its better functioning. To her, the written word was not a way to academic fame (that she deservedly received anyway) but a means to express insights about how humans shape their environment. In fact, if she had lived in a less tumultuous period, she probably would have written less and instead spent more time pottering about in her beloved garden in Aylesbury, or finally realised the dream of buying a small house in Fiascherino on the Ligurian coast that, for its combination of sea, hills, and sun, she grew very fond of in her later life.

So the essays in this volume are *not* a review of Susan's work. Instead, they are a reaction to the provocations with which in her work she knocked a good deal of conventional wisdom about what is going on in the global economy off the shelf. And they are also a reply to her friendly invitation to join in defining promising avenues of future research into what we still do not know about the determinants of stability and instability of global capitalism, and attempts to control it. It is our attempt, therefore, to acknowledge an intellectual debt impossible to repay. It is also an attempt to continue conversations we individually or collectively had the privilege to enjoy with a woman whose contributions to making sense of the contemporary capitalist world will fertilize international political economy and international business studies for a long time. We hope that this book is one Susan would enjoy reading. No doubt she would knock us over the heads for what we got wrong or simply neglected – some things never change.

We do know that she would appreciate the title. In *The Retreat of the State* (1996), Strange self-critically remarked that the title of her earlier – in her own words – anti-textbook, *States and Markets* (1988), was a misnomer. It put too much emphasis on the state even though her analysis showed that non-state authorities played a large, and increasing, part in determining the who-gets-what in international political economy. Retrospectively, '[*M*]*arkets and Authorities* would have been a better title'(1996, x). Her interest in and preoccupation with the power of markets was made clear in the subtitles of her last two books: *The Diffusion of Power in the World Economy* (1996), and *When Markets Outgrow Governments* (1998a).

This introduction has two purposes. First, it introduces the reader to Strange's thoughts about the governance of the global economy, especially financial markets. Second, it relates the six individual essays to the theme of the book and to each other.

SUSAN STRANGE'S WORK: A BRIEF PRIMER

How to Think about the World

States and Markets started out as an attempt 'to synthesize politics and economics by means of structural analysis of the effects of states – or more properly of any kind of political authority – on markets and, conversely, of market forces on states' (1988, 13–14). The enquiry encompassed:

> the social, political and economic arrangements affecting the global systems of production, exchange and distribution, and the mix of values reflected therein. Those arrangements are not divinely ordained, nor are they the fortuitous outcome of blind chance. Rather they are the result of human decisions taken in the context of man-made institutions and sets of self-set rules and customs. (1988, 18)

Security, production, finance, and knowledge are the primary structures of the international political economy. This means that those who offer protection; who decide what shall be produced, and how; who control credit; and who control access to knowledge and ideas, can exercise power. Values refer to the need for security, the want for wealth, preferences regarding justice, and the freedom to choose. A situation, thus, is embedded in structures whose relative importance depends in part on value preferences. It is further described by key bargains that characterise the choices open to government and non-government authorities alike.

> My proposal ... is that you should look for the key bargains in any situation, and then decide which might, and which probably will not, be liable to change, altering the range of choices for all or some of those concerned. (1988, 39)

The Retreat of the State (1996) is a sequel to *States and Markets*. It reiterates, using new illustrations and exploring different theoretical avenues, the thrust of the earlier argument:

> [t]he impersonal forces of world markets, integrated over the postwar period more by private enterprise in finance, industry and trade than by the cooperative decisions of governments, are now more powerful than the states to whom ultimate political authority over society and economy is supposed to belong. (1996, 4)

This does not mean that all responsibilities once discharged by the state are now being taken care of by non-state collectivities. 'The diffusion of authority away from national governments has left a yawning hole of non-authority, ungovernance it might be called' (ibid., 14). In order to understand these changes, we have to broaden our definitions of power and politics. Power is best judged as 'power over' outcomes rather than, as conventionally done, as 'power from' resources or capabilities. Outcomes can be sought after as well as unintended; in the latter case they emanate from 'unconscious power'. For example, the creation of an open world market economy was an aim of US policy. But '[w]hat its policymakers did not fully intend ... was the enhanced power that this would give to markets over governments, including their own' (1996, 29). Politics, too, is about much more than what politicians do. It is about why collectivities form, what consequences their association has while it lasts, and which repercussions are generated as it disintegrates.

> By extending the limits of 'political', we include the notion of a world society that is buffeted and sometimes bruised by both the political system of states and by the economic system of markets. At the least, we should include in the agenda any issue on which some government, or some non-state authority, at some time, has thought it necessary to intervene. (1996, 40)

In case anyone thinks that the recipe for structural analysis makes for a quick, ready-to-cook meal, here are the ingredients:

> The total, aggregated impact of inter-governmental, state and sub-state authority, together with that of diverse non-state authorities is the product not so much of an orderly, static 'regime', as of a complex pattern of interlocking, interacting bargains among them all. These bargains may be relatively stable, or relatively unstable. They are often very vulnerable to changes in technology and changes in the market, in conditions affecting supply or demand. The job of the political economist is to identify, if s/he can, firstly, the points of greatest vulnerability to existing bargains, and secondly, the potential distributional and value-mix consequences of both the existing complex web of bargains and of conceivable alternative webs. (1996, 99)

The Important Issues

Uncontrollable financial markets
Prescience is rare in the social sciences. But not in this case. Editorials critical of uncontrolled capital markets published in the financial press in the wake of the 1997 Asian financial crisis read as though they were lifted straight out of *Casino Capitalism* (Strange 1986). It is important to remember that that book was written prior to the Plaza (1985) and Louvre (1987) Agreements aiming – and failing – to stabilize the dollar exchange rate at a level palatable to the world's major economies; to Black Monday's stock market crash in October 1987; to the Savings & Loan debacle in the US mortgage industry in the late 1980s; to the demise of major international bank houses such as Bank of Commerce and Credit International (BCCI) and Barings; to the coming into fashion of emerging markets; and to Long Term

Capital Management's (LTCM) Fed-supervised bail-out, a major hedge fund with a series of quality-name clients gone bankrupt because of its imprudent investments in high-yield emerging markets in Asia and elsewhere. '[T]he gamblers in the casino have got out of hand, almost beyond, it sometimes seems, the control of governments' (1986, 21). More tentatively than her later work, in this first big shot at international finance after the dissolution of Bretton Woods, Strange asked whether states had become weaker or markets stronger. The subtle answer was that states had become weaker not because markets had encroached upon their territory but because they – especially the US – had made a series of decisions and 'non-decisions' that left markets with more freedom. Thus, whatever the present situation, if financial turmoil is likened to the genie out of the bottle, it was governments who took the cork off. '[M]arkets exist under the authority and by permission of the state, and are conducted on whatever terms the state may choose to dictate, or allow' (1986, 29). The book ended with a prediction that, eleven years later, exactly played out:

> Because of the information problem ... and the ignorance among the controllers and regulators of what the bankers and speculators are up to, it must be expected that we have not seen the last financial scandal or the biggest banking collapse. Another Continental Illinois crisis cannot be ruled out. And the outcome will be the same, that the US government has to take over the liabilities and debts because the consequences for the economy at large of doing otherwise would be too great. The nationalization of banking will be taken a step further. (1986, 192)

The globalization of international finance remained the prime issue of international politics and economics for Strange. For centuries it had been the prerogative of states or central banks to create money. The advent of financial derivative instruments towards the end of the last century effectively turned over some of the power to 'invent' money to the market, especially the banking system. Madness followed on casino's heels. *Mad Money* updated and extended her earlier work (1998a). It did not mince words. Next to long-term environmental degradation, a possible collapse of confidence in the world financial system, causing a credit crunch and economic stagnation, threatens to 'jeopardize civilization and the life chances of our children and grandchildren ...' (1998a, 2). Her review of changes in financial markets since the mid-1980s led to five conclusions none of which are positive:

- '[F]inance calls the tune'. ... The real economy of manufacturing, services like entertainment, tourism, transport, mining, farming and retailing – all of it dances to the fast or slow rhythms of financial markets ... .
- [G]overnments of states have less control over their economies and societies than they had ten, twenty or thirty years ago ... .

- [T]he pace of economic concentration in big business has substantially accelerated ... .
- [M]oral contamination[:] ... Firms that have access to large amounts of credit and that make such large profits can afford to bribe politicians and officials as well as to reward employees ... .
- [T]here are widening income gaps (1998a, 179–81).

Multinational firms and state development strategies

The most prominent non-state authority in Strange's work are multinational firms. In *Rival States, Rival Firms*, co-authored with John Stopford, she argued that structural changes in the world economy have influenced the way states and multinational firms behave, and how they relate to each other (1991). First, where states used to compete for power over more territory, they now compete for the means to create wealth within their territory. Second, the emergence of corporate networks provides incentives for governments to promote location-specific advantages to attract wealth-generating investments. Third, small, poor countries face increased barriers to entry in industries most subject to global competition. Only investment in skills can help them out of the impasse. Fourth, taken together these changes add two new dimensions to traditional inter-state diplomacy: state-firm and firm-firm relationships. Fifth, the increased complexity of relationships has increased the complexities of the agendas to manage both for governments and firms. Sixth, the net total of these shifts is that the volatility of change increases, and that outcomes of the new diplomacy diverge.

> Change in the international political economy points one way: states are losing power to pursue independent policies and now must master the new game of triangular diplomacy. At the same time, the outcomes of the bargaining have been markedly divergent. Indeed, divergence is a *leitmotif* of this book – divergence between continents, between countries in the same continent or region, even within countries over time and among sectors and, finally, divergence between firms – not necessarily in accordance with their national origin. (1991, 29)

Hence the impact on host countries differs, and so does the effect of one firm relative to another.

> The national behaviour and performance of multinationals depends upon their strategies at global and local levels and upon the position of the firm within its industry. The interaction between governments wanting to change firms' behaviour and firms resisting or acceding to pressure throws up a kaleidoscope of responses. The tussles between headquarters and subsidiaries can lead to unexpected outcomes that sometimes help and sometimes hinder host states. We found enormous variation in behaviour on all the issues we have raised among the projects we reviewed, even within an industry. Industry averages thus provide poor guides for how sectoral policy should be implemented in firm-specific bargaining. The questions can only be answered at the level of the enterprise. (1991, 168)

Future research should therefore look at the 'almost infinite variety of negotiated arrangements set up in particular kinds of business in developing countries' (1991, 231).

The losers from globalization

It would be difficult to classify Strange as on the right or on the left. What is certain is that she never signed up to an ideology. It is also certain that she tended to argue against whatever the dominant ideology of the day happened to be. This is because dominance breeds complacency and, worse, contempt. Strange never suffered gladly those who sing the hymns of unfettered globalization and forget that modernisation and progress almost always create losers. Her heart was with the losers. This is perhaps one reason why her later work sounds like a roundabout indictment of contemporary capitalism. But that is a superficial reading. For in many ways, *Rival States, Rival Firms*, is a sympathetic guide to governments of developing countries how to make the most of foreign capital. It also may be true that if the world economy made everybody happy, Strange would not have written any books on international political economy at all. To her, unless there was a problem to address, academic writing had no point. One of the clearest statements indicating her concern with rising inequality is made right at the beginning of her last book.

> My concern, now as it was then, is not technical – with the efficiency of the system – but social and political, with the consequences for ordinary people who have never been asked if they wanted to gamble their jobs, their savings, their income in this casino form of capitalism. (1998a, 3)

Reasons for Hope?

If problems in the real world are the drive behind your analytical instincts, the question then is whether you believe in doom and gloom, or whether you think that there is a way out. On balance, Strange took to the latter. She was convinced that, as most problems were man-made, men and women in principle were able to find solutions. In other words, there was nothing inevitable about how the world economy would develop henceforth, just as there had been nothing inevitable about how it had developed so far. For example, concerning the liberalisation of financial markets she wrote:

> [T]here was nothing predetermined or inevitable about the policy choices made by the United States which have led to a condition of increased monetary and financial anarchy. It surely follows that if there was nothing inescapable about the path to greater anarchy, there is equally nothing impossible about a return journey towards greater order and stability. (1986, 147)

Both *Casino Capitalism* and *Mad Money* are full of proposals how excess volatility due to reckless speculation could be curtailed. They often read like a plea to the US government to accept its responsibility for the world economy at large.

Michel Albert (2001) muses that, with the irrational exuberance that characterised the US for most of the 1990s deflated, both the administration and American society may be readier to consider policies that are globally easier to digest than the massive capital inflow that made the so-called goldilocks miracle possible. But although he also quotes some (soft) evidence that Americans have grown tired of too much liberalism and are rediscovering the purpose of public investments in health care and education, one might be forgiven for taking his (hard) numbers more seriously. Thus, US pension funds own more than a third of the companies quoted on the French stock market, their French equivalents 2 per cent. It would be naïve to believe that this has no bearing on how those companies are run, or indeed on the choices open to any French government, regardless of political *couleur*. If nothing else, this underlines that Human Choice American carries more weight than what the rest of the world thinks or wants.

Strange would probably regard Albert's idea of a possible new dawn for the enlightened discharge of the US's global responsibilities with scepticism. That would not be because she would be unsympathetic if a little more flexibility and liberalism in Europe were matched by a little more security and welfare state in the US. But as a young journalist with just a column or so of newspaper space at her disposal, she learned to distrust fuzzy concepts, such as today's 'Third Way', or yesterday's 'good governance', or the even more worn out 'international economic cooperation' courtesy of G7 summitry. To her, if you couldn't explain in simple terms what you meant, your ideas were positively immature at best, and possibly not very good anyhow. She maintained a healthy intolerance toward undisciplined writings even after her transition to academia greatly expanded the number of words and paragraphs she was allowed and expected to put to paper. That is why her books stand out from the literature. You might disagree with her arguments but at least they were always accessible; nothing obfuscated the message she intended to convey in the way of convoluted delivery. Her other great asset was her sense of pragmatism. Arguing that it was doable for world leaders to reintroduce a greater measure of control and stability into international financial affairs is not the same as claiming that this is likely to happen. Her proposals how to put a halt to the casino and rein in mad money were imbued with the good spirit of wanting to improve how the world is run. They were also based on a no-nonsense, and thus often pessimistic reading of the world around her. It is this combination that makes her arguments so compelling.

Because of her conviction that contemporary affairs could be made sense of only *over time*, Strange looked for insights – and perhaps at times consolation – in historical analyses.

> [T]he relation of market authority to political authority has never been stable for long, and ... at different times and in different places the pendulum has swung away from one and toward the other and back again, often in ways unforeseen by contemporaries. We may not be able as yet to see how exactly this pendulum may swing back in the future from markets to some kind of authority – not necessarily that of territorial states – but history does offer some reassurance that, somehow, sometime, it probably will. (1986, 45)

Her writings do not make clear how likely she thought change for the better is. It is probably fair to say that she felt it would be long in coming. Does that make her an optimist?

OUTLINE OF THE BOOK

In and Out of Fashion: Global Finance and Capital Mobility, Yesterday and Today

Attitudes to international capital flows have changed over time. Both theories about the effects on home- and host-countries of footloose money in search of the highest returns and recurring financial crises have informed what academics and policymakers did and do think about the desirability of capital mobility. In brief, over the past 200 years the pendulum swung from profound scepticism *vis-à-vis* capital account convertibility to advocacy of the most efficient capital allocation regardless of borders. Recently, the 1997 Asian crisis has contributed to a much more qualified and cautious view of the feasibility of capital mobility; thus, at least in some quarters the discussion has come full circle.

The classical economists were never unconditionally in favour of free capital movements. They knew that investments abroad – mostly, in their case, outflows from the UK – could lead to a globally more efficient allocation of resources. But Francesco Asso shows that they cautioned that incomplete information and inevitable speculation would translate into more uncertainty which, in turn, might destroy capital, affect other economies through contagion, and even provoke wars or other political conflicts (Asso, in this volume). From Smith and Ricardo via Mill, Bagehot, Cobden, and, finally, to Marshall, economic thinking implied what Asso calls a 'home bias': if you keep your funds invested at home, your profit rate may be marginally lower. But in exchange your life is going to be easier because you do not have to worry about moral hazard in corporate governance, different rules and customs abroad, and so on. The classical economists concerned themselves not just with the motives of individual investors but also with the perceived gap between private benefits and social costs of capital market integration. Thus, in a memorable quote Bagehot quipped that 'at particular times a great deal of stupid people have a great deal of stupid money'. Stupid, because according to Cobden international credit helps dubious governments to finance their wars. Stupid also, because disappointed investors rely on their home governments to defend their interests in host countries. Both trends augment conflicts in the world – clearly an eminently relevant point for current world affairs as well. At the latest since Mill the classical thinkers knew that international infrastructure projects such as the development of railways required the mobilization of international funds and they also realized that the rise in foreign direct investments was inevitable. But they were adamant that the increase in irrational speculation was part and parcel of financial globalization and that more risk taking would lead to financial instability with ensuing panics culminating in the destruction of capital. Much better known, for the same reasons, Keynes favoured restrictions and control on capital flows, too (Asso, in this volume). The key difference between Keynes and the classics is that the latter believed that home bias was a natural trait of rational economic actors aware of the uncertainties and risks associated with free capital flows. Keynes, by contrast, argued that investors would indeed go for the highest return, regardless of risk, and that governments had to impose restrictions on capital flows to avoid individual speculations leading to full-blown financial crises. The difference is not necessarily philosophical. The classics never lived to experience the events of financial turmoil and worldwide depression that shaped Keynes' thinking.

Hence without being old-fashioned, Strange's criticism of unfettered financial globalization is in the good company of many great minds. And recently, the prevailing consensus in favour of opening up capital markets where they still had been closed, especially in developing countries, has come to be questioned. The reason is, again in line with Strange's warnings, that the ensuing risk of instability is not worth the price in terms of a potentially more efficient global resource allocation. Although recent financial turmoil in Asia and elsewhere was in part homemade in that poor financial regulation and widespread corruption obviously do not help, imperfections in global capital markets clearly have to share in the blame (Obstfeld 1998). Private capital flows that have replaced official funds in all but the poorest countries come with a problematic baggage. First, they are extremely volatile. Under the 1988 Basel Capital Accord, capital adequacy requirements on short-term lending are significantly lower than on long-term lending. This facilitated the undesirable herd behaviour leading up to the 1997 crisis when short-term funds first massively piled in and then massively bailed out, thus exacerbating the imbalances in the external accounts anywhere between Thailand and Brazil (Griffith-Jones and Ocampo 2000, see also Brenner 2001). It was countries like Chile applying unorthodox policies such as reserve requirements on capital inflows that avoided the fall-out from contagion (see Akyüz 2000, for a review of the special problems global financial instability pose for developing countries; also Strange 1998b, especially her summary of a paper by Eatwell (1998); for more on Tobin-type taxes, see e.g. Wachtel 2000).

The second problem of private capital flows to developing countries is that more than four-fifths are concentrated in little more than a dozen middle-income countries plus China. Hence, when things go wrong, the counter-cyclical funding required to address the imbalances is large. This throws up not just the question of whether the international financial institutions have enough funds to stabilize the system. It also means that, at least during and after crises, assistance to middle-income countries may crowd out long-term financing to poor countries (Griffith-Jones and Ocampo 2000). So short of unlikely funding increases the multilaterals and their masters somehow will have to figure out how to involve the private sector in orderly debt work-outs or, yet better, in ensuring as much as possible that private sector behaviour become less crisis-prone (Boorman and Allen 2000).

In international financial reform, it is perhaps clearer what *not* to do than what to do. We are all subject to what Strange called 'areas of significant ignorance'. Yet the debate about integrated financial markets appears to be one whose participants, including individuals at the IMF, no longer all behave as though self-doubt were a foreign concept. That, in itself, is already good news. In Strange's words:

> [A]lthough academic debate by itself rarely changes the basic ideas – whether pro-market or pro-state – that at any time dominate the knowledge structure, academic debate when it takes place against a background of growing disillusion, of doubt and uncertainty can act as a catalyst to action. (1998b)

Global Finance and the US: System Management or (Benign) Neglect?

Strange consistently argued that a system whose most important currency was managed primarily in the national interest, rather than with an eye to international financial stability, is prone to crises. That is why she criticised US policy choices for bringing about conditions that enhanced the volatility of capital markets following the demise of the Bretton Woods system in the early 1970s. In the early 1990s, the US ran a budget deficit to the tune of 4 per cent of GDP. The need to finance this deficit held global currency, equity, and bond markets in thrall as investors wondered how the US government would honour its international obligations other than by continuing to borrow. We now know that the US did in fact manage to end federal profligacy, arriving at a budget surplus. But whether a surplus can be maintained in the face of the Bush administration's 2001 $1,350bn tax-cut package, is anyone's guess. If not, the US government again will have to attract capital inflows with scant regard where these funds might be employed more usefully in other parts of the world.

Charles Kindleberger takes issue with Strange's critique of the role of the US. His discussion of benign neglect focuses on three periods: the demise of Bretton Woods in the early 1970s, the first Reagan administration, and the second Clinton administration in its dealings with Europe. His criticism advances from different angles (Kindleberger, in this volume). First he cautions that people often criticize other countries' policies because they feel compelled to defend their own country's policy choices. This may be the case in general but in her earlier work Strange, a British citizen, had lambasted post-war sterling policy just as much as she later trained her fire on the management of the dollar (1971). Second, Kindleberger argues that the management of the international reserve currency reflects the push and pull of conflicting interests in the US federal (or any other) system of government, rather than a presumed unitary US position. He cites disagreements between the Secretary of the Treasury on the one hand and the Federal Reserve on the other as happened during the abandonment of the dollar-gold parity in 1971. Third, US policy is influenced by the behaviour of other participants in the international system. Thus, if free riding by its partners raises the cost of long-term system maintenance for the US to unacceptably high levels, the latter may be well justified in reverting to a more explicit defence of the national interest. On occasion, national pride or hubris of a country in trouble may prevent its partners, including the US, from extending a helping hand. Fourth, Kindleberger refers to what in international macroeconomics is called the 'inconsistent trinity'. Liberalized capital markets pose constraints on the pursuit of exchange rate and monetary policy. That is, it is impossible for a country with fixed exchange rates and capital account convertibility to orient its monetary policy toward domestic goals. Governments must drop one of these three policy goals to pursue the remaining two (Obstfeld 1998). This is no less true for the US who prioritizes a stable macroeconomic environment and free capital movement, leaving the exchange rate to be determined by its followers. The latter, in turn, cannot pursue an independent monetary policy. 'This division of function is the theoretical justification for the leading reserve currency to neglect its exchange rate' (Kindleberger, in this volume). Finally, charges of US neglect or indifference do not hit the nail on the head if the outcome of such policies appears to be contrary to US interests. In conclusion, Kindleberger holds that the management (and behaviour) of international money is too complex to lend itself to sweeping generalizations. His essay helps to identify avenues for further research that would allow (some) generalizations without diminishing complexity of the world around so much as to get lost in meaningless abstractions.

Global Finance and the Developing World: What Place for the Newcomers?

Disagreements lead to arguments that hopefully fertilize the search for common ground. Kindleberger disagrees with Strange. In the two chapters following his, David Calleo and Jo Lorentzen put a different accent on what hinders the full integration of developing countries into the world economy. In short, Calleo argues that multilateral arrangements cannot accommodate the conflict potential resulting from the huge income gaps between rich and poor countries. He does not believe that the liberal world economy club is ready for new candidate members such as India or China, or that the earth's ecology could sustain the environmental pressures of very large populations in the fast lane to economic growth. By contrast, Lorentzen lambastes governments in the advanced economies for shortchanging developing countries in the world trade system and argues that disingenuous implementation of global accords on trade, investment, and the environment exacerbates the plight of the poor.

What does all this have to do with global finance? Calleo (in this volume) hones in on the role of the US in the international financial system. The system so far largely proved resilient to breakdowns, the ultimate casino scenario. It managed to contain the worst effects of recurrent financial crises because it was organized around the double (or triple) role of the US: as a lender and buyer of last resort who arranged bail-outs when necessary, and as a protector who exchanged military security for its allies against their willingness to underwrite its deficits. Calleo doubts that this arrangement is sustainable in the post-cold-war world. With the Soviet threat gone, Europe is much less dependent on US military protection. By implication, it is also less willing to finance the very deficits without which the US cannot fulfill its role as lender or buyer of last resort. For example, with fiscal deficits gone for the time being, the main reason for the US current account deficit is that the US acts as the buyer of last resort for Asia, where recovery from the 1997 crisis depends on exports. This has become more difficult through the arrival of China (and the slowdown especially in the US IT sector) who outcompetes the other second-generation tigers. Calleo argues that China's increasing share in world production and trade was, along with the dollar appreciation, one of the key reasons why East Asian manufacturing industries had got into trouble in the first place, triggering withdrawal of portfolio investments and, thus, the currency crisis. With Japan unable to absorb East Asian exports to the extent required for a recovery, the US continues to be the buyer of last resort, but only if European capital also keeps financing its resulting trade deficit which Calleo thinks it will not.

The ultimately unsustainable current account deficit and the fragmentation of the US government along with the growing influence of special interest groups in the US Congress that defy and handicap an internationalist perspective on the world, sap the country's ability to lead an increasingly diverse world. Unfortunately, no alternative arrangement for a more or less orderly running of the show is in the offing. This is why the world is not up to the challenge of accommodating large numbers of partly very talented but overall very poor people. China's aspirations to match its absolute weight with per-capita incomes suited for an emerging superpower implies a more aggressive competition for the world's resources, with very undesirable environmental consequences. The likely concentration of China's and India's economies on industry and agriculture would considerably change the character of global output – from lighter to heavier – with attendant consequences for global warming. To Calleo, the extension of western life styles to the rest of the world would be their very undoing. The logic is essentially Malthusian – in a shrinking theatre even the well-heeled guests cannot cling to their front-row seats forever. So instead of a casino that explodes due to the financial merry-go-round we sit in one that implodes thanks to a combination of overcrowding and unsustainable consumerism. The best that could happen in terms of a cleaner world would be for the advanced economies to set a positive example of more responsible resource management.

Jo Lorentzen also addresses the relationship between rich and poor countries, and people, in the global economy. His chapter takes its inspiration from Strange's concern with the losers in the global casino, and from her contention that markets have become more important than public authorities in determining the who-gets-what in the global distribution of resources (Lorentzen, in this volume). He identifies as losers all those who live in abject poverty and who have little prospect of taking advantage from the global integration of markets. While he acknowledges that poverty has many determinants, he singles out the trade and investment policies of advanced economies as major culprits. The one-sided and hypocritical implementation of global accords such as the Uruguay Round package reflect the differential bargaining power of rich vs poor countries. Hence, at the same time as developing countries go through the tedious process of adapting and harmonizing national legal provisions with international rules on, for example, intellectual property rights, the rich countries continue to stall on, or implement half-heartedly, market access provisions aimed at allowing entrepreneurs in poor countries to exploit their competitive advantages.

Lorentzen focuses on protectionism in agriculture and textile and leather goods. He also reviews the rich countries' abysmal record of condoning clandestine immigration to satisfy demand in industries as diverse as fruit picking and prostitution while refusing to grant migrant workers minimum protection and basic rights. Lorentzen does not dispute Strange's general contention that states willingly or unwillingly have passed power to markets. But he argues that in an era of liberalized market access – key for developing country growth and not sufficient but necessary condition for poverty alleviation – rich country governments call the shots. Hence they, and not some impersonal private authority, are to be blamed for giving hundreds of millions of people a hard time, and global integration a bad name.

Global Finance and Redistribution: Markets and Authorities in the Future

Markets generally are good at producing efficient outcomes. Or, at least, for some things. Leaving everything to the market may be the best way of making the best refrigerators or the best eggs available at the best possible price, and even speculative futures markets for eggs can be useful in warning the hens in timely fashion when they are about to saturate the market. But markets in money, especially in long-term-future claims on money – money to be spent in one particular currency or another – are a very different matter. Dore looks at pensions in this light. Most continental European and Japanese 30-year-olds can, under present arrangements, look forward to getting a pension in 40 years' time which depends on the willingness of the then 30-year-olds to pay taxes and social security contributions, just as it is their current contributions which support today's 70-year-olds – a state-collectivist version of the peasant household where those in their prime work and consume, and those past their prime only consume. The trouble with this pay-as-you-go system is that the numerical balance of workers and pensioners is changing.

By some projections, half a century from now in the rich countries there will be about as many people over 65 as those aged between 20 and 64. In Italy and Japan, the ratio is projected to go as high as two-thirds. Ageing and lower fertility rates will reduce the ratio of people in employment to every elderly person from five in 1960 to an estimated two in 2030. With increasing life expectancy, this means that both public pension payments and health care spending will rise, putting pressure on public finances. The OECD estimates that fiscal balances could deteriorate by some 5 per cent of GDP over the next 50 years and that sooner (in Japan) or later (in Europe and the US) public debt would rise rapidly. Health spending could rise to 8 or 9 per cent of GDP from its current level of 6 per cent (Visco 2001). It appears that something will have to give, for in the absence of higher labour utilization rates or productivity boosts simply proscribing the current arrangement, neither guarantees an adequate retirement income for the aged nor keeps the tax burden of the active population within acceptable limits. Unless something compensates for the contracting labour force, living standards will fall. The general policy consensus is that this 'trouble' is insuperable; that pay-as-you-go systems have to be drastically cut back and that the alternative is markets. Workers' contributions go into an individual fund which is invested according to the individual's choice among standard alternatives, and pensions depend on the future value of the financial claims thus bought.

The empirical core of Dore's chapter is a description of Japanese debates about the introduction of such a defined contribution scheme. In the course of it he makes several points. First, if you take the possibilities of economic growth into account, the difficulties of maintaining the pay-as-you-go scheme may be much exaggerated – particularly, with understandable enthusiasm, by the financial services industry. Second, the social cohesion which the pay-as-you-go system entails is morally valuable and worth preserving, not least because a certain amount of income redistribution is possible within it, whereas the shift from state to market pensions would simply reproduce, and probably exacerbate, the inequalities which the labour market itself is increasingly producing. Reducing risk-sharing devices is likely to create extreme winners – people who reach middle age with the world in their pockets – and extreme losers – for example people whose employer responded to technological change by relocating production, thus depressing the value of their home equity and diminishing their chance of a decent and dignified retirement (cf. Shiller 2001).

His discussion arises from and relates to Strange's work in two respects. First, if all the OECD countries were to fund market pensions on the scale of the US and Britain the world would be awash with capital, the volatility of financial markets would be vastly increased, rates of return would fall – and in the end the pensioners would be cheated. Second, these changes in pension arrangements bear very much on the possibility of reintroducing capital controls which has been discussed since the Asian crisis. One could just about imagine, contemporary Japan opting out of full participation in global financial markets. For a future Japan in which the financial services industry is as dominant as such a shift in pension funding would make it, the option would almost certainly be politically foreclosed.

Louis Pauly gropes for elements of a theory that would assist in the search for conceptual alternatives to the current arrangement of global capitalism (Pauly, in this volume). He addresses the conceptual and practical relationship between authority – power based on legitimate rule – and power based on coercion. The former is associated with national governments or other local authorities looking out for the societies whose interests they were elected to safeguard. The latter emanates from liberalized markets, especially the fragmentation of control over monetary policy, whose workings may have profound cross-border effects and effectively constrain or contradict the policies of public authorities, especially of weaker countries. As opposed to the postwar compromise of 'embedded liberalism', in modern forms of global governance the principle of unconstrained individual wealth maximization substitutes nationally legitimated and internationally coordinated social welfare policies – instead of societies based on the principle of solidarity, understood as the willingness to share the costs of economic change, we get groups of people both within and across societies that benefit from liberalization and technological innovation, and groups that don't. In other words, there are both winners and losers. The winners have the power; what do they do with it? And what of the political authority that previously guaranteed and organized the compact behind embedded liberalism which ensured that there wouldn't be too many losers?

Pauly argues that the power of markets remains unconstrained only in normal times. Normal times are different from moments of crisis. In normal times, markets deliver the goods and take the credit for it. Those who benefit, have a ball. Those who don't, refrain from spoiling the party because that is not what one can do in 'normal times'. In moments of crisis, markets wreak havoc but blame (national and supranational) authorities for the resulting mess. Crises catalyse political legitimacy of public authorities both because policymakers are determined to control the damage and because market participants look to them to do exactly that. Hence, allegations of the demise of public authority are contingent on things going well. Whether this fundamental insight into the character of global finance continues to hold, depends on the degree to which the undisputed expansion of markets reaches a point of no return beyond which solutions to crises become technically and politically impossible. Technically, because the fixers – as in pre-Putin Russia – are in the pockets of the plutocrats, and politically, because no one else is in charge. In turn, this depends on whether people, losers and non, allow this to happen or whether they demand of their political authority to put an end to it.

How to make sense of all this? Unresolved differences between visions of a rule-based, liberal world order moulded by the US and concepts of a more equitable distribution of the world's resources within and across countries fuel all major conflicts in the global economy. How these conflicts are addressed and managed (or fail to be either) indicates if some new form of global authority capable of controlling the casino comes into being, and what shape it might take. Pauly implicitly takes issue with the message in Calleo's and de Cecco's (de Cecco, in this volume) hardnosed views of what alternative arrangements are feasible. He suggests that supranational organizations as mediators may reconcile market integration with local – national or regional – preferences that put a high value on tangible and intangible assets that survive only if they are protected against unconstrained competition. The question thus becomes whether there can be a second incarnation of 'embedded liberalism', with more supranational interlocutors – including NGOs – than before and who would be behind bringing it about.

So what?

In short, this book is about the demerits of unrestrained international capital flows and the effects they have on human lives in the global economy. It discusses the key role of the US in current and alternative forms of system management, both economic and political. It analyses what prospects the global economy holds for those that are weak, or latecomers, or otherwise disadvantaged. And finally, it speculates what kinds of national or global authority would manage to address the shortcomings of the system in terms of greater financial stability and a more equitable distribution of resources. The contributions throw open many questions which this introduction pointed to. For answers, however tentative, read on.

ACKNOWLEDGEMENT

Ron Dore and Francesco Asso provided very useful comments that much improved the final version of this introduction. Many thanks to both of them.

REFERENCES

Akyüz, Yilmaz (2000), 'On Financial Instability and Control' in Jan Joost Teunissen (ed.) *Reforming the International Financial System*, pp. 164–77. The Hague: Fondad.
Albert, Michel (2001), 'Capitalismo contro capitalismo: Dieci anni dopo', *Il Mulino* 50, no. 3.
Boorman, Jack, and Mark Allen (2000), 'A New Framework for Private Sector Involvement in Crisis Prevention and Crisis Management' in Jan Joost Teunissen (ed.) *Reforming the International Financial System*, 101–23. The Hague: Fondad.
Brenner, Menachem (2001), 'The Varying Nature of Volatile Forces. Mastering Investment Part Seven', 6–7, Supplement to *Financial Times*, 25 June.

Eatwell, John (1998), 'International Financial Liberalisation: The Impact on World Development'. United Nations Office of Develoment Studies. UNDP, reprinted from 1996 working paper. Quoted in Strange (1998b).

Griffith-Jones, Stephanie, and José Antonio Ocampo (2000), 'Facing the Volatility and Concentration of Capital Flows' in Jan Joost Teunissen (ed.) *Reforming the International Financial System*, pp. 31–63. The Hague: Fondad.

Obstfeld, Maurice (1998), 'The Global Capital Market: Benefactor or Menace?' *Journal of Economic Perspectives* 12, no. 4: 9–30.

Shiller, Robert (2001), 'A Safety Net for Our Future', *Financial Times*, 12 January, 17.

Stopford, John, and Susan Strange, with John Henley (1991), *Rival States, Rival Firms*. Cambridge: Cambridge University Press.

Strange, Susan (1971), *Sterling and British Policy: A Political Study of an International Currency in Decline*. London: Oxford University Press.

Strange, Susan (1986), *Casino Capitalism*. Oxford: Blackwell.

Strange, Susan (1988), *States and Markets*. London: Pinter.

Strange, Susan (1996), *The Retreat of the State: The Diffusion of Power in the World Economy*. Cambridge: Cambridge University Press.

Strange, Susan (1997), 'The Future of Global Capitalism; Or, Will Divergence Persist Forever?' in Wolfgang Streeck and Colin Crouch (eds) *The Political Economy of Modern Capitalism*, pp. 182–91. London: Sage.

Strange, Susan (1998a), *Mad Money: When Markets Outgrow Governments*. Ann Arbor: University of Michigan Press.

Strange, Susan (1998b), 'What Theory? The Theory in *Mad Money*', Working Paper no.18/98, Centre for the Study of Globalisation and Regionalisation, University of Warwick.

Teunissen, Jan Joost (ed.) (2000), *Reforming the International Financial System*, The Hague: Fondad.

Visco, Ignazio (2001), 'Paying for Pensions: How Important Is Economic Growth?' OECD, mimeo.

Wachtel, Howard (2000), 'Tobin and Other Global Taxes', *Review of International Political Economy* 7, no. 2: 335–52.

1. The 'Home Bias' Approach in the History of Economic Thought: Issues on Financial Globalization from Adam Smith to John Maynard Keynes

Pier Francesco Asso

It may still be wise and prudent statemanship to allow the game to be played, subject to rules and limitations, so long as the average man, or even a significant section of the community, is in fact strongly addicted to the money-making passion.
John Maynard Keynes, *The General Theory of Employment, Interest and Money* (1936)

MR KEYNES AND THE CLASSICS ON CAPITAL MOBILITY

'Let goods be homespun ... and, above all, let finance be primarily national' (Keynes [1933] 1971–89, XXI, 236). With this outcry in times of deep economic recession, financial crashes and heavy unemployment, John Maynard Keynes attacked what he thought to be another cornerstone of the mainstream tradition in economics. Ten years had passed since Keynes had demonized the role of gold as a 'barbarous relic'; eight since he had dismissed sterling's return to a fixed parity as a deleterious decision taken by a pompous man who was exclusively interested in the City's financial prestige. The theoretical appeal of money neutrality – embedded in Say's law of macroeconomic equilibrium – had already been disputed in his early writings on international monetary reform, and he was ready to fight the final struggle against monetary orthodoxy in order to rescue mankind from 'the confusions of the Quantity Theory of Money which once entangled me' (Keynes [1936] 1971–89, VII, xxxiv).

The opportunity to control foreign investments and international capital movements was just another of his 'early beliefs' which Keynes faithfully maintained throughout his life. World War I had drastically interrupted the process of financial integration while all postwar attempts to restore it had

20

failed to reproduce stability, confidence and prosperity. Ideas, knowledge, art, hospitality, travel: these remained, for Keynes, the 'things which should of their nature be international' (Keynes [1933] 1971–89, XXI, 236), but, so he warned in 1933, government intervention ought to minimize the risks of systemic crisis which are inevitably associated with the development of an integrated capital and credit market. Too much finance was an outstanding fault of modern societies, which generated unbearable costs in terms of greater uncertainty, instability and asymmetric behaviours. Up until his very last days, Keynes discussed it in connection with unemployment, the domestic rate of interest and an unequal distribution of world income.[1]

The dilemma of perfect capital mobility came to be integrated in the development of Keynes' theoretical contributions and policy proposals after Versailles, until it was ruled out from the formal model of the *General Theory*. His *Treatise on Money* – which he conceived and wrote in times of financial euphoria and sent to the publishers immediately after the Crash – provided the main theoretical arguments against financial globalization. There Keynes placed special emphasis on the destabilizing consequences of speculative capital movements from one country to another. The proliferation of competitive financial centres even in continental Europe had increased the likelihood that small changes in confidence or interest rate differentials induced abnormally large movements of funds. This required constant supervision and immediate responses from central banks which, under fixed exchange rates, had inevitably lost much of their influence over the domestic rate of interest. Exchange rate misalignments and the pound overvaluation had brought about the collapse of foreign investments in Britain and stimulated the participation of British money to the development of the Wall Street bubble. Criticism of the gold standard rules was also levelled on the grounds that the asset market and the output market did not adjust with the same speed: international capital movements reacted to interest rate differentials much faster than commodity trade did to exchange rate changes. While debating the transfer mechanism with Bertil Ohlin, Keynes stressed that international finance rather than commodity trade set the tune of the economic cycle.[2] As a consequence of political and institutional developments, confidence in domestic monetary policy and the efficiency of the credit system was shaken: an increase in the money supply was often followed by a speculative movement that produced a net capital outflow, thus bringing about instability and welfare losses.[3]

Differences in the speed of adjustment and nominal flexibility had been ignored by traditional quantitative theory, but were relevant for policy proposals. As possible remedies, Keynes believed in controls and government intervention to curb excessive integration of capital markets. In *The End of Laissez-Faire*, he called for 'some coordinated act of intelligent judgement' which predetermined the 'desirable' amount of domestic savings and, more significantly, 'the scale on which these savings should go abroad in the form of foreign investments' (Keynes [1926] 1971–89, IX, 292). In the *Treatise on Money* he suggested that overshooting and investment volatility may be offset by restrictions on capital movements, a widening of the gold points, or indirect taxation on foreign bonds so that domestic investments could be indirectly subsidized and rendered a more stable function of income (Keynes [1930] 1971–89, VI, 280ff).

In the emergencies, outright exchange control was preferred to a differential taxation of foreign bonds because the latter was difficult to implement: credit was 'like water ... it may be used for a multiplicity of purposes ... and will remorselessly seek its own level over the whole field unless the parts of the field are rendered uncompromisingly watertight, which in the case of credit is scarcely possible' (Keynes [1930] 1971–89, VI, 285). In a long-term perspective the first best solution was to go beyond national sovereignty. Ever since the end of the 1920s Keynes preached for the foundation of a world central bank, whose liabilities were to be accepted on the same terms of gold by member central banks. The new institution would also supervise the establishment of more symmetric behaviour in the adjustment of the external account – Keynes' greatest concern being with creditor countries unwilling to lend or duly expand their economy.

In times of mass production, large-scale investments and the growing legal intricacies of modern corporations, free capital mobility also generated asymmetric information by increasing the gap between real ownership and the effective responsibility of management. This, as Berle and Means (1933) had shown, was a serious phenomenon within a country, because lenders and investors 'lack altogether both knowledge and responsibility towards what they momentarily own' (Keynes [1933] 1971–89, XXI, 236). However, Keynes stressed that the real dangers arose once this feature of modern capitalism became global: 'when the same principle is applied internationally, it is, in times of stress, intolerable' (Ibid.). In fact, the efficiency gains from portfolio diversification were largely offset by the unmeasurable risk burdens associated with asymmetric information. Defaults and repudiations, in fact, induced a worsening in international relations and a breach with moral laws, which went well beyond the individual welfare gains:

> There may be some financial calculation which shows it to be advantageous that my savings should be invested in whatever quarter of the habitable globe shows the greatest marginal efficiency of capital or the highest rate of interest. But experience is accumulating that remoteness between ownership and operation is an evil in the relations between men, likely or certain in the long run to set up strains and enmities which will bring to nought the financial calculation. (Ibid.)

Finally, Keynes had little faith in increasing returns and thought that, after the wake of successful innovations which had produced the second industrial revolution, the advanced nations could gain little from economies of scale and a more global division of labour. True, after Versailles, he was hesitant to suggest the abandonment of free trade and never advocated quantitative restrictions, retaliations or the revival of new mercantilist policies. He still paid respect to the moral virtues of the free trade dogma that he once had learnt at Eton or Cambridge. Nevertheless, by 1933 he believed that the era of classical free trade was definitely over and solemnly declared: 'I am no longer a free trader ... to the extent of believing in a very high degree of national specialization and in abandoning any industry which is unable for the time being to hold its own' (Keynes 1971–89, XII, 193; XX, 379).

But was free trade really an indisputable dogma for nineteenth century classical economists? Moreover did free trade apply only to commodities, or did the principle really need to be extended also to capital and other productive factors? Was, as Keynes believed, financial integration and perfect capital mobility a real cornerstone of classical economics, even if one agreed with his rather extensive definition of the school?[4] What kind of awareness did 'pre-Keynesian' economists show toward the development of a global capital market?

Jacob Viner and Lionel Robbins did some pioneering work on these topics at about the same time when Keynes voiced his pleas for a greater 'National self-sufficiency'. Following their path, many authors have agreed that classical economists did not constitute a homogeneous sect proposing general laissez-faire as an indisputable dogma.[5] Undoubtedly, with the British economy at the back of their mind, Smith and Ricardo had provided convincing arguments that free trade was the optimal policy in terms of a more efficient allocation of resources and for its long-term prospects of growth. In his effort of systematization of received doctrines, John Stuart Mill had then acknowledged that a free international intercourse of economic relations ought to become the worldwide 'rule', even though, as a rule, it admitted several exceptions. Indeed, most economists belonging to the British classical school deserve the credit for having formulated such exceptions with greatest clarity, remarkable farsightedness, and analytical accuracy: it was in fact Adam Smith who, in the *Wealth of Nations* (*WN*), had put forward the strategic argument for protection, when he wrote that 'defence was more important of opulence' or supported Cromwell's decision to discriminate against Dutch shipping; it was major Robert Torrens who preached for strict reciprocity and country discrimination in trade policy and, more significantly, defined the rationale for an 'optimal' tariff policy which brought about superior welfare gains rather than a static adoption of free trade; it was finally John Stuart Mill himself who, following again Smith and a longstanding non-British tradition, cautiously approved the protection of infant industries, introducing dynamic arguments, economies of scale and the strategic importance of the economies of learning.

Certainly, for the nineteenth century economist, 'real' trade issues had paramount importance for the development of new analytical techniques, the formulation of policy advice, and for increasing his professional reputation within society. However classical economists did not disregard, as is often thought, the issue of capital mobility or the development of international financial relations which increasingly gained importance around the London money market. They realized that private capitals generally moved without restrictions, and increasingly flowed into bonds financing long-term government debt, railroads and other infrastructure projects. They knew that financial globalization accompanied and, to some extent, eased the growth of the nineteenth century international economy and the spread of industrialization. They recognized that financial integration began well before 1800, and it particularly affected Northwestern Europe, the former British colonies and the regions of recent settlement. They repeatedly saw that, in times of war or political strain, the scale of capital flows increased significantly: during the Napoleonic Wars, for example, foreign capitals moved out of British government bonds and played a key role in the 1797 Bank of England restriction of sterling convertibility (see Neal 1990; Bordo et al. 1998).

On many of these new features of the international economy Smith, Ricardo, Mill and their contemporaries offered scattered but sometimes illuminating remarks. In this respect, this essay aims to prove that the classical economists' support for perfect capital mobility was much more conditional and critical than their 'realistic' support for free trade. Undoubtedly, as many authors have already argued, many classical economists simply assumed the argument away, having built their 'free trade rule' on the premise that productive factors had a 'natural' tendency to remain completely immobile between countries. Discussion of capital movements was marginal, unsystematic, and developed mainly in connection with the balancing of external payments. Following David Hume and the report of the Bullion Committee, capital flows were a key factor in the market-induced adjustment process or occurred as a once-for-all unilateral transfer of purchasing power occasioned by such asymmetric shocks as war reparations, crop failures or other exceptional events. In describing the price-specie-flow mechanism, Hume – and, with few exceptions, all those who followed his approach – declared his faith in the flexible smoothness of the process and essentially disregarded the asymmetric nature of inflation and deflation. Therefore, in an ideal market economy, capital movements were by no means a disturbing factor but, on the contrary, guaranteed the short-term stability of the external accounts and increased the allocation efficiency of the real productive forces.

However, the assumption of capital immobility was made (by David Ricardo) mainly for analytical reasons, that is for the inherent logical coherence of the idea of comparative advantages and the doctrine of international values. In all cases whenever, even in Ricardo, the assumption was relaxed, international capital mobility was viewed with little sympathy, occasional fears, profound scepticism and good reasons for control and outside intervention. Moreover, if free international trade was considered tantamount to an economy-wide productivity gain, the same was not thought of capital movements and financial integration. For the nineteenth century classical economist a regime of perfect financial globalization often failed to pass a cost-benefit test for reasons which the reader may find recurrent in contemporary literature and are even beginning to creep into the official reports of international institutions. Increased uncertainty, lack of information, hazardous speculation, destruction of capitals, losses from overtrading and contagion, more destructive wars and political conflicts, were among the negative externalities which were often associated with the international spread of financial integration.

Thus, with different emphasis, in the writings of classical economists one can often find a strong 'home bias' in favour of domestic investment. The integration of capital markets had quite a low place in their scale of preferences. They repeatedly argued that its sacrifice would insure a higher growth of the domestic capital stock, of the military power and of the political security of the nation-state. On this viewpoint, the gap between the classics and Keynes was much narrower than the latter would have been ready to admit. In their writings one can find a presumption that for the greater stability and security of the economic system individuals should not diversify in order to maximize returns. As is emphasized in recent literature (Lewis 1999; Okina et al. 1999), investors simply should – and, as a matter of fact, do – continue to prefer to hold as little of their wealth as possible in foreign assets.

Thus, as Lionel Robbins put it in his LSE lectures, Ricardo *regretted* the international movement of capital and labour (Robbins 1998, 211, emphasis in original): just another idiosyncracy for a man whose ancestors came from Portugal, Italy and Holland and whose profession and personal fortune had been built as a stockbroker. In what follows, we shall try to investigate the reasons of 'Ricardo's idiosyncrasy' against mad money.

ADAM SMITH ON THE 'HOME BIAS APPROACH'

When Adam Smith wrote the *Wealth of Nations*, there were no intimate connections between different national markets for short-term funds or more long-term investments. However, citing different historical circumstances, Smith noted the growing intensity of international capital mobility and took into careful consideration investors' decisions to make direct investments abroad. What were – according to the founder of modern political economy – the opportunity costs and the repercussions of foreign investments on the rate of profit and the more general prospects of the British economy?

In the real world, Smith observed, labour immobility was certainly a more visible phenomenon than capital immobility: 'man is of all sorts of luggage the most difficult to be transported' (*WN*, I, viii, 31). On the contrary, in modern commercial societies, one could detect an increasing relationship between international trade of goods and the export of capital. The entrepreneur had a 'natural' instinct to reason in terms of his industry rather than of political geography. In one famous passage of the *Wealth of Nations*, Smith offered the remark that 'a merchant ... is not necessarily the citizen of any particular country. It is in a great measure indifferent to him from what place he carries on his trade' (*WN*, III, iv, 24).

However, referring to the nature of the new mercantile system, Smith saw quite unfavourably the emergence of completely mobile capital in the hands of the merchants who seem 'to have no fixed or necessary residence anywhere'. For the economy as a whole, home ought to become the 'natural' centre of gravitation and attraction of new capital investments:

> Home is in this manner the centre, if I may say so, round which the capitals of the inhabitants of every country are continually circulating, and towards which they are always tending, though by particular causes they may sometimes be driven off and repelled from it towards more distant employments. (*WN*, IV, ii, 6)

In economic terms, preference for domestic investments was effective 'upon equal or nearly equal profits' (*WN*, IV, ii, 6), even because 'a very trifling disgust will make him remove his capital, and together with it all the industry which it supports, from one country to another' (*WN*, III, iv, 24).

What were for Smith the reasons why capitalists should naturally reveal home preferences, particularly in the presence of a differential rate of profit which should stimulate capital exports and arbitrage opportunities?

First of all, Smith thought that information and transaction costs would drastically be reduced by geographical proximity: 'in the home trade his capital is never so long out of sight as it frequently is in the foreign trade'. Besides, access to information was easier at different stages of the value chain. The investor ran smaller risks of imperfect knowledge, because he 'can know better the character and situation of the persons whom he trusts' (*WN*, IV, ii, 6), and if he should happen to be deceived, 'he knows better the laws of the country from which he must seek redress' (Ibid.). With domestic investments, the capital costs of monitoring and supervising one's employees were also reduced while the whole society was facing lower costs of external intervention.

Second, 'home bias' indirectly guaranteed the production of such public goods as greater security and stability. Investors, Smith often repeated, always considered both security and returns, and domestic investments generally produced a more balanced combination of both. Thus, security considerations exerted a determinant influence on the rate of domestic investment and the level of capital formation. Now, unlike shipping or even foreign trade, foreign direct investment was not a 'routinized' activity, so that security considerations could not be reduced to some form of objective commercial risk which follows 'a strict rule and methods' (*WN*, V, i, e, 32 and 34).[6]

Most interestingly, even the famous 'invisible hand' passage was specifically written to relate 'home bias' and domestic investments to national security, rather than, as many have argued, to discover a perennial property of the market economy. There, Smith specified that, unexpectedly, beneficial outcomes occur if investors show a preference for holding their wealth in secure, domestic assets.[7] The 'invisible hand' had nothing to do with the efficiency of markets in allocating resources: it was a force that contributed to the security of the nation by retarding the export of capital (Persky 1989); it was the inducement that a merchant had to keep his capital at home, thereby increasing the domestic stock of capital and enhancing military power, 'both of which are in the public interest, and neither of which he intended' (Grampp 2000; Khalil 2000). This choice will then prove to be advantageous for society and for the wealth of our nation. This was 'the beneficial end it [the invisible hand] promotes, and is the only end he explicitly names' (Grampp 2000).

Third, it must be remarked that Smith nowhere seems to believe that a greater international diversification of assets could provide a powerful engine of growth. In a natural order, Smith suggested that capital should first favour domestic agriculture and become planted in the soil. To avoid the decline in the wealth of our nation, England ought not follow the example of the Hanseatic League. Capital should be employed either in buildings, or in the lasting improvements of lands: 'no vestige now remains' – he reminded his readers – 'of the vast wealth said to have been possessed by the greater part of the Hanse towns' (*WN*, III, iv, 24). Recent history provided numerous examples which ought not to be imitated by Britain. The Dutch – Smith recalled – preferred to put their wealth into French and English public debt and, what was worse, began to lend 'great sums to private persons in countries where the rate of interest [wa]s higher than in their own' (*WN*, I, ix, 9–10). Particularly these decisions served the needs of 'private traders and adventurers of foreign countries' and were quite detrimental to the maintainance of Dutch commercial superiority.

Fourth, the international spread of financial capitalism may also have an indirect impact on wars and international conflicts. Smith had ambivalent views on this point. On the one hand, he described England's success in fighting wars with the aid of Dutch financiers. The network of credit and the widespread use of foreign bills of exchange allowed the British government to transform 'wool into mercenaries' with no great outflows of gold (*WN*, IV, i, 29). On the other, had such borrowing facilities not existed, he bluntly stated that 'wars would in general be more speedily concluded and wantonly undertaken' (*WN*, V, iii, 51).

Finally, the increasing trend toward international investments and modern forms of business organization led to the separation between the act of saving and the act of investment which, in their turn, brought about an increased frequency of 'moral hazard' situations. According to Smith:

> the directors of such companies, however, being the managers rather of other people's money than of their own, it cannot well be expected that they should watch over it with the same anxious vigilance with which the partners in a private copartnery frequently watch over their own ... Negligence and profusion, therefore, must always prevail, more or less, in the management of the affairs of such a company. It is upon this account that joint stock companies for foreign trade have seldom been able to maintain the competition against private adventurers. (*WN*, V, i, e, 18)

Insecurity and uncertainties of this kind, Smith noted, would sooner or later help restore mercantilistic practices, economic crimes of all sorts, or require the presence of a very 'visible' intervention from the outside: 'they have accordingly very seldom succeeded without an exclusive privilege; and frequently have not succeeded with one'. (Ibid.)

ADAM SMITH ON CAPITAL MOBILITY, SPECULATION AND RISK MANAGEMENT

In the *Wealth of Nations*, Smith shows increasing awareness of the risks which might be determined by the emergence of mercantile interests and a more competitive society. Unlike Ricardo, for Smith the real enemies of progress and growth were not the remnants of landowners' interests but the perverse (and unforeseeable) effects generated by the new kinds of business misconduct. More than by a declining rate of profit, capital accumulation was checked by profit-driven speculative activities – and foreign direct investments fell within this category. Capital mobility entailed the risk of greater speculation and net wealth losses for the community. While Smith believed that merchants had often an irrational confidence in their own fortune and capacity, he attached a negative premium on excessive risk taking. An occupation offering a small chance of attaining a high position and a large income will yield a lower average return than one in which earnings happen to be more uniform.

Throughout the *Wealth of Nations* hostile words are addressed to adventurers and projectors who, unlike the 'prudent' capitalist, are driven by the desire to obtain high profits and undertake risky speculations which often end with a considerable loss of capital. Smith's 'prudent man' is wise, a close observer of facts, and acquires command over new wealth without taking excessive risks. Society needs to be protected from investors in very risky or speculative ventures (West 1990).

Home bias was thus independent from investors' optimism about domestic returns. Quite the contrary. Whenever profits are too high, all the sober virtues of a mercantile society – beginning with parsimony – tend to disappear. For Smith the successful investor must then decide to invest at home and escape all temptations of easy profits which could be obtained by capital diversion. With low international diversification, capital accumulation grows even in the presence of a falling rate of profit. This occurs, provided that the ratio between productive and unproductive labour is raised:

> the demand for labour increases with the increases of stock whatever be its profits; and after these are diminished, stock may not only continue to increase, but to increase faster than before ... a great stock, though with small profits, generally increases faster than a small stock with great profits. Money, says the proverb, makes money. (*WN*, I, ix, 13, 14)

To protect the prudent behaviour of the investor Smith envisaged the possibility of restrictions on the level of profits. Far from being an exception to the system of natural liberty, such restrictions would fall within the proper realm of government intervention, and were left to the 'wisdom of future statesmen and legislators to determine' (*WN*, IV, vii, c, 61). Smith gave numerous examples in the field of commercial and banking law. Some of which, such as the imposition of a legal rate of interest, were directly meant to favour a more extensive access to credit particularly by such groups as small firms and sober investors which would otherwise be discriminated by the actions of speculative projectors.

Risk considerations were again prominent in Smith's deliberations on interest rate regulations and credit rationing. Speculative projectors may have to be legally restrained in order to reduce the occurrence of moral hazard and adverse selection: 'where the legal rate of interest is fixed but a very little above the lowest market rate, sober people are universally preferred, as borrowers, to prodigals and projectors' (*WN*, II, iv, 15) (see Endres 1996). If otherwise rates were allowed to go higher:

> the greater part of our capital ... would be lent to prodigals and projectors, who alone would be willing to give this high interest. Sober people ... would not venture into the competition. A great part of the capital of the country would thus be kept out of the hands which were most likely to make a profitable and advantageous use of it, and thrown into those which were most likely to waste and destroy it. (*WN*, II, iv, 15)

On the contrary, loans made for low profit home investments generate external economies because of the effects on capital formation and economic growth.

Failure of speculative activities produces a wastage of capital and the dangerous phenomenon of 'propagation'. Smith argues that the financial system as a whole experiences some sort of 'distress' which tends to propagate itself rapidly. In the *Wealth of Nations*, several cases of financial bubbles are discussed and Smith underscores the faults of central banking lending practices: as a result the British economy was at one point thrown into 'clamour and distress'. And the 'real distress' of the country threatened not only the credit of the projectors; more crucially the 'public credit' was placed in a 'parlous' situation (*WN*, II, ii, 71 and 72).

Smith had no doubts that propagation effects must be checked by active government action even if this entailed a virtual violation of man's natural liberty: this principle of intervention applied to physical as well as to economic security that, sometimes, could be threatened by the application of free banking or perfect capital mobility.

Compared to an interest-bearing loanable fund, Smith also revealed strong preferences for the 'superior security of land' (*WN*, II, iv, 17). Capital that was invested in any country by commerce and manufacturers 'is all a very precarious and uncertain possession, till some part of it has been secured and realised in the cultivation and improvement of its lands' (*WN*, III, iv, 24). As a store of value, land ownership not only involved lower economic risks of capital loss, but also entailed greater protection from institutional uncertainties. Capital was always there, visible and tangible. Conversely, returns on foreign investments also depended, according to Smith, on 'elements of human folly and injustice ... in distant countries (where there are people) ... whose character and situation' are not fully understood.

Finally, the purchase of foreign stocks might also offset the action of the wise legislator at the detriment of society. To avoid the burden of high taxation, capital will easily move out of the country rendering more problematic the implementation of domestic policy:

> land is a subject which cannot be removed, whereas stock easily may. The proprietor of land is necessarily a citizen of the particular country in which his estate lies. The proprietor of stock is properly a citizen of the world, and is not necessarily attached to any particular country. He would be apt to abandon the country in which he was exposed to a vexatious inquisition, in order to be assessed to a burdensome tax, and would remove his stock to some other country where he could either carry on his business or enjoy his fortune more at his ease. (*WN*, V, ii, f, 6)

Being a penetrating observer of human and business psychology, Smith concluded that investors were, both as a group and individually, hardly careful or rational: they often tended to overestimate their own luck and the value of their opinions about the future. Risk-carriers were generally over-optimistic until losses began to outweigh gains. He wrote of the 'overweening conceit which the greater part of men have of their own abilities' and concluded that the 'chance of gain is by every man more or less overvalued and the chance of loss is by most men undervalued' (*WN*, I, x, b, 26). Again intervention and wisdom were needed to secure capital growth from subjective risks.

DAVID RICARDO AND THE RATIONALE FOR PERFECT CAPITAL IMMOBILITY

In his celebrated chapter on foreign trade, David Ricardo recognized that, unlike interregional exchange, the international division of labour did not bring about a uniform rate of profit. In his 'corn model', the intersectorial equality of the rate of profit served as a formal abstraction which certainly did not apply whenever markets were segmented by oceans or the national borders. Transportation costs, international conflicts and 'home bias' increased the difficulty of international capital mobility: 'the termination of the war has so deranged the division which before existed of employments in Europe, that every capitalist has not yet found his place in the new division which has now become necessary' (Ricardo [1817] 1951, I, 90).

In Ricardo's *Principles*, the rationale for capital immobility is again explained as a consequence of investors' choice rather than with trade policy attitudes or institutional constraints. English capitalists were well aware that they could reap higher returns on their investments in other countries because of different labour productivity. Ricardo himself, after a successful experience as a stockbroker, was well acquainted with the existence of arbitrage opportunities and interest rate differentials. Nevertheless, in the *Principles* Ricardo wrote that capitalists naturally resisted portfolio diversification and chose to invest in England. In so doing they acted rationally and followed sound motivations. Among them he emphasized 'the fancied or real insecurity of capital, when not under the immediate control of its owner, together with the natural disinclination which every man has to quit the country of his birth and connexions' (Ricardo [1817] 1951, I, 136). Thus, also for Ricardo 'home bias' was mainly determined by greater insecurity, more costly access to information and the obvious discomfort associated with a foreign government, new habits and new laws. Threatened by a declining rate of profit at home, security, ease of supervision and greater knowledge were more relevant economic weapons to wage war against the spectre of the stationary state.

Ricardo was even more radical than Smith in advocating 'home bias' and in his assumption that national entrepreneurs were performing as non-competing groups in the global arena. He repeatedly mentioned investors' loyalty to one's nation among the reasons which induced a merchant to keep his capital at home (an inclination 'which I should be sorry to see weakened') (Ricardo [1817] 1951, I, 136). Moreover, while Smith opted for domestic investments whenever the merchant faced 'about equal or nearly equal profits', Ricardo said that home bias was effective even if returns on overseas investments were 'considerably' more advantageous. Capital export – he critically remarked in his 'Notes on Bentham' – had always detrimental effects on growth and would tend to weaken Britain's manufacturing superiority:

> it can never be allowed that the emigration of Capital can be beneficial to a State. A loss of capital may immediately change an increasing state to a stationary or retrograde state. A nation is only advancing whilst it accumulates capital ... England even if she received the revenues from the capitals employed in other countries would be a real sufferer. (Ricardo [1810] 1951, III, 274)

Discussing trade policy issues, besides producing negative welfare effects, Ricardo argued that indirect taxation on foreign commodities would bring about adverse movements of capital. Increased impediments on essential goods were a powerful stimulus to international capital diversion and the reduction of the domestic capital stock. With restrictive tariff legislation, we offer an 'irresistible temptation to capitalists to quit this country, that he may take their capitals to places were wages are low and profits high'. Inducement to capital exports provided a further argument for Ricardo's radical campaign against the protection of landowners' interests: 'to give a moderate advantage to one class, a most oppressive burthen must be laid on all other classes'. Something that Ricardo was not willing to conceive or actually implement.

Following Smith, in Ricardo we find again a tradeoff between greater financial integration and the successful management of economic policy. If capitals were allowed to migrate freely, individual countries would lose some of their capacity to manage their tax rates effectively. Ricardo, who, having stated it, immediately rejected the 'Ricardian equivalence' between debt and tax finance, warned that the expected future tax burden accompanying a high public debt would induce 'the rich and his capital' to emigrate (Ricardo [1817] 1951, I, 247–49). As a member of Parliament, he constantly advised Government against the imposition of excessive rates of taxation on capital. Tax rate differentials would tempt the investor to 'remove himself and his capital to another country where he will be exempted from such burthens'. Sooner or later, Ricardo warned, this temptation may become 'at least irresistible and overcome the natural resistance which every man feels to quit the place of his birth, and the scene of his early associations' (Ricardo [1817] 1951, I, 248). As a remedy for the huge public debt accumulated in wartime, he preferred more drastic remedies, like the imposition of a levy on all forms of real and financial property. Unlike all alternative procedures of debt consolidation, a capital levy would not induce capital flight, provided that the capitalist community believed the sacrifice to be once for all and non-recurrent (Asso and Barucci 1988; Eichengreen 1990).

Finally, Ricardo had ambivalent attitudes towards technical progress following the introduction of more sophisticated methods of production. They greatly depended on the adverse short-run effects of machineries on labour employment and the wage fund. In a Parliamentary speech Ricardo admitted that 'they operate prejudicially to the working class' (Ricardo [1815–23] 1952, V, 302–3). One of the reasons why, in the end, capital-intensive productions ought to be encouraged was that, otherwise, domestic investors would be incentivated to leave the country. The creation of a new breed of global merchants delocalizing their production lines in neighbouring states would, according to Ricardo, make matters worse for both our national welfare and the labouring class:

> the employment of machinery could never be safely discouraged in a State, for if a capital is not allowed to get the greatest net revenue that the use of machinery will afford here, it will be carried abroad, and this must be a much more serious discouragement to the demand for labour, than the most extensive employment of machinery. (Ricardo [1817] 1951, I, 396)

All things considered, 'by investing part of a capital in improved machinery, there will be a diminution in the progressive demand for labour; by exporting it to another country, the demand will be wholly annihilated' (Ricardo [1817]

1951, I, 397). Following Ricardo, in the age of classical economics a ban on the export of machinery was shared by many who on other issues were fond of using laissez faire slogans and free trade rhetoric.

However, among his closest associates, some began to doubt the validity of Ricardo's 'home bias approach': Ramsay MacCulloch was probably the first, when he quite ironically asserted that 'love of country has its limits', while 'love of gain is a no less powerful and constantly operating principle'.[8] John Stuart Mill accepted the cogency of this criticism but also provided new arguments to the 'home bias approach'.

JOHN STUART MILL: A COST-BENEFIT APPROACH TO FINANCIAL GLOBALIZATION

Having inherited from Jeremy Bentham a strong faith in utilitarianism, John Stuart Mill shared a very optimistic view on the positive effects of free trade and the removal of trade barriers. Mill believed that integration and liberalization would ultimately bring about a real international harmony of interests, happiness of mankind, greater wisdom and world peace. In his writings, economic prosperity was often intended as a means for more universal ends, 'a necessary,condition and an indispensable machinery' of the moral civilization of the universe.

Compared to his famous predecessors, Mill devoted more attention to the issue of international capital integration. By the time he wrote his *Principles of Political Economy,* the importance of capital exportation was a 'fact now beginning to be recognized' (Mill [1848] 1965, III, 515) and Mill approached the issue in terms of benefits and costs. Among the former, Mill was less cautious in establishing strong connections between integration of capital markets and economic growth. If free mobility was granted, resources would be allocated more efficiently, relaxing constraints on the accumulation of funds. On the costs side, Mill observed that as investment opportunities increased, profit margins squeezed and interest rate differentials narrowed: a rational response of the capitalist was the flight toward speculation and investments in emerging, distant markets. Globalization thus stimulated appetites of investors for 'something foreign' and more risky undertakings. In Mill, high returns were often identified as a premium for unmeasurable risk, a point that was later more fully developed by Frank Knight (Knight 1921).

More than Smith or Ricardo, Mill also recognized that, on many accounts, countries were different and so would be the effects from a greater integration of their capital markets. In his analysis, Mill more clearly distinguished between capital exporting and capital importing countries, even though he was obviously more inclined to discuss the former.

In many respects, Mill thought that all countries would derive benefits from global capitalism. There was no nation, Britain included, which did not need to borrow from others: 'the railway operations of the various nations of the world may be looked upon as a sort of competition for the overflowing capital of the countries where profit is low and capital abundant ... The English railway speculations are a struggle to keep our annual increase of capital at home; those of foreign countries are an effort to obtain it' (Mill [1848] 1965, III, 750). For the new developing countries with a low accumulation of savings and backward financial markets, the introduction of foreign capital, was likely to procure both static and dynamic gains. Most interestingly, he put special emphasis on the latter: in fact, it rendered 'the increase of production no longer exclusively dependent on the thrift or providence of the inhabitants themselves', while it also 'places before them a stimulating example ... by instilling new ideas and breaking the chain of habit' (Mill [1848] 1965, III, 186–7, 963). For Britain and the other advanced nations, Mill thought that the globalization of capital could help solve such structural problems as the Malthusian spectres, the 'iron' law of wages, and the deterioration of the terms of trade. For them, 'the export of capital served the national interest' as the importation of foreign goods did in the early stages of industrialization. Mill followed Wakefield and his group of colonial reformers who insisted that capital exports could be a remedy and a relief against a sudden decline in the rate of profit on behalf of a more balanced rate of growth: 'colonization, in the present state of the world, is the best affair of business in which the capital of an old and wealthy country can engage' (Mill [1848] 1965, III, 963). Exported capital may serve to promote the production abroad of cheaper raw materials, foodstuffs, or manufactures for which the more advanced countries provide ready markets, or to develop markets for the export goods of the home market. These benefits will tend to diffuse themselves among all classes in the capital exporting country:

> It is to the emigration of English capital that we have chiefly to look for keeping up a supply of cheap food and cheap materials of clothing, proportional to the increase of our population; thus enabling an increasing capital to find employment in the country, without reduction of profit, in producing manufacturing articles with which to pay for this supply of raw produce. Thus the exportation of capital is an agent of great efficacy in extending the field of employment for that which remains: and it may be said truly that, up to a certain point, the more capital we send abroad, the more we shall possess and be able to retain at home. (Mill [1848] 1965, III, 746)

Therefore, for mature economies, the free access to international capital markets was the most effective way to fight a declining rate of profit, an excessive formation of capital and the stationary state:

the perpetual overflow of capital into the colonies or foreign countries, to seek higher profits than can be obtained at home [has] ... been for many years one of the principal causes by which the decline of profits in England has been arrested. (Mill [1848] 1965, III, 746)

On the contrary, the cessation or prohibition of capital exports enhanced the tendency of a fall of the rate of profit: 'no more capital sent abroad for railways or loans; no more emigrants taking capital with them, to the colonies, or to other countries; no fresh advances made, or credits given, by bankers or merchants to their foreign correspondents' (Mill [1848] 1965, III, 739). Finally, delocalizing capital would help offset Britain's problems with land scarcity and decreasing returns in agriculture: 'if our population and capital continue to increase with their present rapidity, the only mode in which food can continue to be supplied cheaply to the one is by sending the other abroad to produce it' (Mill [1848] 1965, III, 745).

Mill also wrote extensively about the interrelationship between commodity trade and capital movements. Mill recognized that the elasticity of capital movements with respect to interest rate differentials was much more significant than the way commodity trade reacted in response to relative price movements: 'the passage of the precious metals from country to country is determined much more than was formerly supposed, by the state of the loan market in different countries and much less by the state of prices' (Mill [1848] 1965, III, 515). In a later (1865) edition of his *Principles of Political Economy*, Mill added that financial globalization and perfect capital mobility would ultimately bring about worldwide equalization in the rate of profit. He thus agreed with Göschen's statistical findings, that risk or political factors were negligible:

> the loan market of the whole commercial world is rapidly becoming one. The rate of interest, therefore, in part of the world out of which capital most freely flows, cannot any longer remain so much inferior to the rate elsewhere, as it has hitherto been. (Mill [1848] 1965, III, 652f; also quoted in Hollander 1985, 645f)

In the same context, however, while discussing the effects of capital exports on growth, Mill analysed the mechanism of speculation and the formation of expectations. In so doing, Mill gave a heavy blow to traditional classical mechanics, when he argued that the future depends on the idea that men have of it, rather than being determined by the present: if consumers believe prices will rise and act accordingly, prices will rise; if depositors panic and run on a bank, they will induce the realization of these fears.

Therefore, following Tooke's analysis of the London money market, Mill associated greater mobility of investments to speculation. The globalization of capital generated financial instability and other degenerations of economic behaviour. In his studies on commercial crisis and monetary policy, Mill put great emphasis on such phenomena arising from foreign investments as rash speculation, overtrading, revulsions and panics. In these stages of the business cycle, and 'in the commercial revulsions by which such times are always followed', the exportation of capital for foreign investment, was theoretically equivalent to a 'waste of capital' (Mill [1848] 1965, III, 741). Capital flight was an exogeneous shock which inhibited the good functioning of the economic system: 'it does what a fire, or an inundation, or a commercial crisis would have done: it carries off a part of the increase of capital from which the reduction of profits proceeds' (Mill [1848] 1965, III, 746).

Now Mill believed that modern capitalism constituted the ideal environment for these speculative excesses. Among its 'natural' laws one could enlist the efficient production of irrational behaviour and a greater frequency of failures:

> such vicissitudes, beginning with irrational speculation and ending with a commercial crisis, have not hitherto become less frequent or less violent with the growth of capital and the extension of industry. Rather they may be said to have become more so: in consequence, it is often said, of increased competition; but as I prefer to say, of a low rate of profit and interest, which makes the capitalist dissatisfied with the ordinary course of safe mercantile gains. (Mill [1848] 1965, III, 718)

'Mad money' was thus a typical by-product of mature economies: growing capital accumulation at home and periods of business quiescence tended to depress the rate of profit and to stimulate cyclical 'fits of speculation' and capital flight. The possessor of capital was thus tempted 'to incur hazards in hopes of a more considerable return' (Mill [1848] 1965, III, 651). Speculation also induced damaging imitative behaviours:

> the diminished scale of all safe gains, inclines people to give a ready ear to any projects which hold out, though at the risk of a loss, the hope of a higher rate of profit; and speculations ensue, which, with the subsequent revulsions, destroy or transfer to foreigners, a considerable amount of capital, produce a temporary rise of interest and profit, make room for fresh accumulation, and the same round is recommenced. (Mill [1848] 1965, III, 742)

Thus, while John Stuart Mill disagreed with Ricardo's 'home bias approach' he refined Smith's prophecies on the development of a speculative spirit and excessive risk-taking. He perceived that 'home bias' and financial globalization were not alternative regimes, but simply two different, often sequential, phases of modern capitalism. Economic growth had inevitably produced greater integration in the global market. Capital exports promoted, rather than retarded, growth via increased demand for domestic goods. Colonization was the safest way to allocate surplus capital. Nevertheless, the development of an integrated capital market remained associated with increased risk and speculation which generated seeds of destruction. Therefore, the issue of financial globalization inevitably imposed, for the economist and the policymaker, challenges and dilemmas of a theoretical and empirical nature. Mill however closed his chapter on international trade with a note of optimism which again shows his early awareness that a new spirit was beginning to emerge: 'capital is becoming more and more cosmopolitan; there is so much greater similarity of manners and institutions than formerly, and so much less alienation of feeling, among the more civilised countries, that both population and capital now move from one of those countries to another on much less temptation than before' (Mill [1848] 1965, III, 230). Residual constraints to perfect mobility were of an objective and technological nature and no longer belonged to a political, institutional or psychological level: 'to France, Germany or Switzerland [British] capital moves perhaps almost as readily as to the colonies: the differences of language and government being scarcely so great a hindrance as climate and distance' (Mill [1848] 1965, III, 230).

WALTER BAGEHOT AND RICHARD COBDEN ON FINANCIAL GLOBALIZATION

Walter Bagehot was probably the first economist who saw the emergence of a new class of global capitalists and who introduced the idea of a cosmopolitan loan fund from which different countries could draw.

In his *Economic Studies*, Bagehot gives a vivid description of the emerging class of financial capitalists who developed new instruments for the transfer and the accumulation of wealth. Following Smith, Bagehot argued that a cosmopolitan capitalist 'was devoid of national sentiment' and, like a soldier, wielded 'a cosmopolitan loan fund which runs everywhere as it is wanted, and as the rate of interest tempts it' (Bagehot 1880, 67ff). The global capitalist had managed to maintain control over distant assets and to produce a new commodity, 'one of the greatest growths of recent times', which he makes use of 'to aid these operations'. Bagehot neutrally called it 'interest-bearing documents', which however was meant to represent an increasingly wide range of financial liabilities. They included 'the securities of all well-known countries, their national debts, their railways shares and so on [which] are dealt in through Europe on every stock exchange'. Their creation, Bagehot noted, had important effects for the increase of the wealth of nations:

'such interest-bearing documents are a sort of national 'notes of hand' which a country puts out when it is poor and buys back when it is rich' (Ibid.).

International mobility of capital was thus essentially greater than supposed by earlier writers. Bagehot predicted that the economist's distinction between internal and external mobility of capital would soon be found to rest on no enduring foundation. Movements of financial funds, he argued, were beginning to act as substitutes for international gold flows. This was the most important evidence that capital will tend to become internationalized and to move freely in response to slight changes in prices, exchange rates, or interest rates. A rise in profits now attracted capitals almost simultaneously.

Using a Ricardian approach, Bagehot observed that countries were not in the same position in the access to the cosmopolitan loan fund. They had different comparative advantages according to their past economic performance, the rate of saving and the development of financial institutions:

> we must not, however, fancy that this puts all countries on a level, as far as capital is concerned, because it can be attracted from one to the other. On the contrary, there will always tend to be a fixed difference between two kinds of countries. The old country, where capital accumulates, will always, on an average, have it cheaper than the new country, which has saved little, and can employ any quantity. (Bagehot 1880, 67ff)

What tended to become common to all countries was, again, the development of a 'speculative nature' and the creation of a 'speculative fund', which was mainly composed of 'the savings of men of business' (Ibid.).

Therefore, Bagehot recognized that 'the emigration of young men with English capital is one of the great instruments of world wide trade and one of the binding forces of the future'. For a new phase of more widespread economic growth, the international mobility of capital was doomed to play the same role that the development of a domestic banking system had done for the first industrial revolution:

> in this way the same instruments which diffused capital through a nation are gradually diffusing it among nations. And the effect of this will be in the end much to simplify the problems of international trade. But for the present, as is commonly the case with incipient causes whose effect is incomplete, it complicates all it touches. (Bagehot 1880, 67ff)

Also for Bagehot, one possible complication was represented by the increase of speculation. Sooner or later speculation will feed panic and capital destruction. Mill's words were almost literally reproduced, albeit in a less detached way:

much has been written about panics and manias, much more than with the most
outstretched intellect we are able to follow or conceive; but one thing is certain,
that at particular times a great deal of stupid people have a great deal of stupid
money ... At intervals, from causes which are not to the present purpose, the
money of these people – the blind capital, as we call it, of the country – is
particularly large and craving; it seeks for someone to devour it, and there is a
'plethora'; it finds some, and there is a 'speculation'; it is devoured, and there is a
'panic'.[9]

Quite unexpectedly, among Bagehot's contemporaries, an attack against
financial cosmopolitanism, came from one of the leaders of the Manchester
School, Richard Cobden. In fact, as far as trade policy was concerned,
Cobden systematically rejected all the exceptions to free trade put forward by
the classical economists, and particularly those elaborated by Torrens, Mill
and MacCulloch. Cobden repudiated both the principles of reciprocity and
gradualism, which Ricardo had also admitted in his public battles against the
corn laws and sterling inconvertibility. He disregarded Britain's possibilities
of introducing an optimal tariff in virtue of her monopolistic capacities and
was profoundly shocked by John Stuart Mill's openings on behalf of the
protection of infant industries.[10]

In their speeches, Bright, Cobden and Gladstone promised a train of
universal prosperity and peace to follow from the adoption of free trade.
Laissez-faire, they argued, was sound in economics, politics and morals.
However, exponents of the Manchester school in the nineteenth century, like
the Whigs in the eighteenth century, were rather inclined to disparage all
movements of productive factors. Here, again, the national sentiment
prevailed. The American trade seemed to divert labour and capital that could
be usefully employed on English soil, without conferring any compensating
advantage. The slave trade, on the contrary, found favour with many because
it would prevent the draining off of Englishmen and lessen the danger of
establishment of a competitive industry.

Moreover, unlike international trade, financial integration was not
conducive to peace but often served as an instrument of power policy and
'stock jobbing' imperialism. Cobden established close connections between
the rise of financial globalization and such threats that may jeopardize
civilization as the outbreak of international conflicts. In their double position
of investors and financial dealers, Cobden feared that capitalists were in a
unique position to manipulate the policy of nations and destroy democracy:

we want to prevent lending money to those bankrupt governments, in order that
they may keep soldiers ... loans are often applied under the pretence that it was
wanted for a railway ... it was raised to pay for the atrocities perpetrated in the
Hungarian war, not from the savings of the Barings or the Rothschilds, for they are
not the people who lent the money, but for the small capitalists in England, who

have small savings and who wish to get 5 instead of 4% ... I was asked whether I, as a free trader, was consistent with my principles when I denounced this use of money? I was told that a man had a right to lend his money without inquiring what it was wanted for ... I say that no man has a right to lend money if he knows it to be applied to the cutting of throats. (Cobden 1850, 418)

Within British economic thought, these arguments against global finance were later developed in Hobson's writings on imperialism. Hobson singled out the growing cosmopolitanism of capital as the most important economic factor in imperialism. Speculation and manipulation of values formed the ganglion of international capitalism. Financial capitalism also involved greater economic and 'moral' risks because governments became identified with investors who had an easy task to manipulate ministers and politicians to protect their interests in case of need. Private investors, Hobson argued, felt assured that, should things turn bad, the national government would intervene in their defence:

Investors who have put their money in foreign loans upon terms which take full account of risks connected with the political conditions of the country, desire to see the resources of the government to minimise these risks and so to enhance the capital value and the interest of their private investments. The investing and speculating classes in general have also desired that Great Britain should take other foreign areas under her flag. (Hobson 1938, 56)

HOME BIAS IN THE AGE OF VICTORIA: ALFRED MARSHALL

Alfred Marshall restated the classical case for 'home bias' in a typical Ricardian fashion. Risk factors, the national sentiment, information and transaction costs made home investments economically more convenient. In *Money, Credit and Commerce*, Marshall acknowledged that, compared to the classical age, opportunities for portfolio diversification had greatly augmented. However, the economist advised the investor to consider other factors than yield differentials. It was indeed becoming:

easier and safer than formerly to invest capital in foreign countries; but of two investments of equal intrinsic merits, one at home and the other abroad, the former has still a great balance of pecuniary advantage as well as of sentimental attractiveness. For information with regard to it is more easily obtained and more easily tested; the income from the investment is drawn with less trouble and expense; and if any hitch arise with regard to the recovery of the capital itself in due time, the commercial and the legal difficulties of the task are likely to be much greater if the capital is invested abroad than if it is invested at home. (Marshall 1923, 9)

In his early essays, Marshall had stated this point with even greater conviction:

> a man will not in general invest capital in any commercial undertaking in a foreign country unless he expects to obtain thereby a rate of interest considerably higher than he could derive from a similar undertaking in his own country ... at least sufficient to compensate him for the extra risk, trouble and expense which the investment occasions to him. (Marshall [1879] 1975, 20)

Foreign investments entailed higher information and transaction costs, due to the difficulties of repatriation or settlement: the investor willing to operate in foreign markets 'can obtain only imperfect and tardy information about the persons and the circumstances whose movements affect the undertaking and ... he cannot rapidly withdraw his capital and apply it to meet any new emergency' (Marshall [1879] 1975, 20).

Marshall also attached special weight to the difficulties of attaining reliable information on the real destination of domestic savings. Indeed, by the end of the nineteenth century, after the first important episodes of international debt crisis, many studies had come out to show that foreign defaults were hardly more frequent than defaults on domestic securities (Lehfeldt 1912–13). However, asymmetric information was considered to be another fundamental cause of market segmentation. Marshall believed that – apart from government and railway loans – new foreign capital issues were characterized by an insufficient degree of transparency and good collateral. He feared that the range of financial claims that were traded internationally might broaden and even include all sorts of private liabilities. Government bonds and public utilities, in fact:

> impose slight difficulties if compared with those which hinder a man from forming an estimate of the value of private securities which may be offered by individuals resident in distant countries ... capitalists are unwilling to undertake much trouble in the supervision of petty loans to people whose affairs are not open to ready inspections. (Marshall [1879] 1975, 21)

Marshall also distinguished between the destabilizing effects of portfolio investments and the growth potentialities of foreign direct investments. Among the reasons why capitalists undertake the latter, great emphasis was put on market enlargement and efficiency-seeking activities. On these matters, British economists began to express mixed feelings of fear and admiration for what other countries were doing. In particular, due to its superior technical skills and education system, it was frequently anticipated that Germany would soon acquire a comparative advantage in attracting these kinds of investments at the expense of Britain. Free capital movements and the capacity to attract foreign direct investments would complete the relative retrogression of British economy. Again it was Walter Bagehot who observed that, in terms of annual flows:

> young men also now transfer their capital from country to country with a rapidity formerly unknown. In Europe perhaps the Germans are most eminent in so doing. Their better school education, their better-trained habits of learning modern languages and their readiness to bear the many privations of a residence among foreigners, have gained them a prominence certainly over the English and the French, perhaps above all other nations. (Bagehot 1880, 70–71)

Nevertheless Ricardo's belief that comparative advantages were statically allocated among countries still had a part in the economic writings at the end of the century. As far as financial globalization was concerned, England retained some superiority for its greater stock of disposable capital and, above all, for the more advanced technical skills of the City's network of international financial intermediation. Moreover, at least in the short run, 'their language is the language of the great commerce everywhere and tends to become so more and more' (Bagehot 1880, 70–71).

CONCLUSIONS

This chapter took its inspiration from reading *Casino Capitalism* and *Mad Money* (Strange 1986, 1998). In *Casino Capitalism*, Susan Strange blames contemporary academic economists for their uncritical and dogmatic approach toward the issue of greater capital market integration. In *Mad Money*, she observed that a greater understanding in the technical working of the global financial system still prevented political economists from grasping the economic, political and social damages caused by price volatility, market instability and erratic behaviours. Consequently I began to wonder what could we have to learn on these matters from the academic community of the past: was financial globalization a subject on which those who contributed to build up today's mainstream had little to say or did they simply assume it away in their strenuous efforts to shed light on the real driving forces of modern capitalism?

Both *Casino Capitalism* and *Mad Money* contain passages where Susan hints at those few thinkers of the past who raised critical concerns against the virtues of perfect capital mobility and grim predictions for the more general national (and global) welfare. With the sole exception of Chicago's Frank Knight, Susan concluded that one had to search outside orthodoxy, or even outside economics, to find some illuminating critical voices against the dangers of *Mad Money*.

In this chapter, I have tried to show that, on the contrary, great economists of the past, from Adam Smith to Alfred Marshall, watched with mixed feelings the prospects of greater capital mobility and foreign investments. I have also argued that, at least from a normative standpoint, John Maynard Keynes might have found good company in his life-long struggle against uncontrolled financial globalization. True, for quite a long time, international trade and international capital movements were not approached in an integrated manner by economic theorists and remained two distinct features of which the former maintained paramount importance, at least in the long run. Nevertheless, following Adam Smith, in the early stages of nineteenth century economic integration, economists saw reasons of conflict between the mutual gains from trade and the potential losses engendered by growing capital outflows. While commodity trade was quite often seen as being equivalent to a net productivity gain and a powerful chance for development, foreign investments came to be identified as a net drain of resources, as a source of imprudent speculations and excessive risk-taking, ultimately leading to a decrease of domestic capacity and to crisis propagation. In other words, for society at large, they were a rather costly undertaking for which no invisible hand could conceivably burst in to everybody's rescue.

Classical economists put great emphasis on some burdensome costs of exchange (or transaction costs, as they have come to be defined) which were typically associated with the rise of financial capitalism. Potential investors were subject to information costs, to a greater frequency of unmeasurable subjective hazards, to institutional problems of different nature, not to mention the difficulties related to the legal system, the political system, the educational system, the cultural environment of societies. Smith and Ricardo warned that foreign investments may also become a source of insecurity, declining loyalty and weakened national pride. Among their detrimental consequences, they listed the possibility of more cruel and longer wars, of easing the propagation of financial distress and bring about forms of adverse selection, since imprudent investors were those who most eagerly sought out risky loans, whatever their cost. When financial integration became more widespread, nineteenth century economists also began to question the existence of a strong relationship between foreign investments and the domestic growth of income and employment, and still continued to attach some positive importance to the survival of a distinct 'home bias'.

Among the possible remedies against the shortcomings of financial globalization, nineteenth century economists were, as one might expect, quite optimistic in the response of human action. Radical government intervention was hardly ever invoked, even though some exceptions can be found in the fields of credit rationing and optimal taxation. Apart from these features, public authorities were asked to play a passive role. In fact, the 'home bias' sentiment against capital diversification was the natural and desirable consequence of investors' rational choice – a positive conclusion which John Maynard Keynes was quite unwilling to subscribe for the post-Versailles world.

While many of the costs of financial globalization are obviously lower today than at the times of Smith and Ricardo, Susan taught us that their relevance is undiminished while strong remains the need for positive action coming from both authorities and organised individuals. In fact some of the problems Smith and his followers had envisaged for global finance can be held directly responsible for the recent wave of financial crises and for the change of attitudes which many analysts at the highest institutional quarters held toward the desirability of unfettered capital mobility. At least in this sense, IMF economists ought not to fear committing any breach with orthodox economic thought from Adam Smith to John Maynard Keynes.

ACKNOWLEDGEMENT

I wish to thank Luca Fiorito and Jochen Lorentzen for most valuable comments on a previous version of this essay.

NOTES

1. 'Advisable domestic policies might often be easier to compass, if, for example, the phenomenon known as 'the flight of capital' could be ruled out' (Keynes [1933] 1971–89, XXI, 236).
2. 'Historically the volume of foreign investment has tended to adjust itself – at least to a certain extent – to the balance of trade rather than the other way round, the former being the sensitive, the latter the insensitive factor' (Keynes 1971–89, XI, 475).
3. 'If English investors, not liking the outlook at home, fearing labour disputes or nervous about a change of government, begin to buy more American securities than before, why should it be supposed that this will be naturally balanced by increased British exports? For, of course, it will not. It will in the first instance, set up a serious instability of the domestic credit system – the ultimate working of which it is difficult or impossible to predict ... If it were as easy to put wages up and down as it is to put the bank rate up and down, well and good. But this is not the actual situation. A change in international financial conditions or in the wind and weather of speculative sentiment may alter the volume of foreign lending, if nothing is done to counteract it, by tens of millions in a few weeks. Yet there is no possibility of rapidly altering the balance of imports and exports to correspond' (Keynes [1930] 1971–89, VI, 300).
4. In a letter to Roy Harrod, Keynes observed that 'freedom of capital movements is an essential part of the old laissez faire system and assumes that it is right and desirable to have an equalisation of interest rates in all parts of the world. In my view the whole management of the domestic economy depends upon being free to have the appropriate rate of interest without reference to the rates prevailing elsewhere in the world. Capital control is a corollary to this' (Keynes 1971–89, XXIII).
5. See, among others, Bloomfield (1994) and Irwin (1996). Particularly Bloomfield contains an illuminating chapter on the relationship between international capital movements and

growth in classical economists, which has been very useful in the preparation of this chapter.

6. The always 'very modest profits of insurers' is the result of low risk or alternatively high security (*WN*, V, i, e, 34).
7. 'By preferring the support of domestic to that of foreign industry, he intends only his own security ... and he is in this, as in many other cases, led by an invisible hand to promote an end which was no part of his intention' (*WN*, IV, ii, 8).
8. MacCulloch (1824). In their private correspondence this issue had already been discussed. In his reply to MacCulloch's scepticism, Ricardo reaffirmed the point: 'I have always said that the desire to stay in our own country is a great obstacle to be overcome' (Ricardo [1819–21] 1952, VIII, 357).
9. Bagehot, 'Essay on Edward Gibbon', quoted by Kindleberger (1978), p. 1.
10. 'I believe that the harm which Mill has done to the world by the passage in his book on *Political economy* in which he favors the principle of protection in young communities has outweighed all the good which may have been caused by his other writings' (quoted in Irwin 1996, 128–9).

REFERENCES

Asso, P.F. and E. Barucci (1988), 'Ricardo on the National Debt and its Redemption: Some Notes on an Unpublished Manuscript'. *Economic Notes*, (2), 5–36.
Bagehot, W. (1880), *Economic Studies* edited by R.H. Hutton, London: Longmans.
Berle, A.A. and G. Means (1933), *The Modern Corporation and Private Property*. New York: Macmillan.
Bloomfield, A.I. (1994), *Essays in the History of International Trade Theory*. Aldershot: Edward Elgar.
Bordo, M.D., B. Eichengreen and J. Kim (1998), 'Was There Really an Earlier Period of International Financial Integration Comparable to Today?', NBER Working Paper Series, n. 6738, September.
Cobden, R. (1850), 'Speech Before the Peace Society', Wrexham, reprinted in John Bright and James E. Thorold Rogers (eds), *Speeches on Questions of Public Policy*, London, 1870, vol. II, 405–410.
Eichengreen, B. (1990), 'The Capital Levy in Theory and Practice', in Rudiger Dornbusch and Mario Draghi (eds), *Public Debt Management: Theory and History*. Cambridge: Cambridge University Press, pp. 191–223.
Endres, A.M. (1996), 'Security' and Capital Formation in 'The Wealth of Nations', *History of Economic Ideas*, **IV**, (1–2), 149–73.
Grampp, W. (2000), 'What Did Smith Mean by the Invisible Hand?', *Journal of Political Economy*, **108**, (3), 441–65.
Hobson, J.A. (1938), *Imperialism*. 3rd edn, London: Macmillan.
Hollander, S. (1985), *The Economics of John Stuart Mill*. 2 vols, Oxford: Basil Blackwell.
Irwin, D. (1996), *Against the Tide. An Intellectual History of Free Trade*. Princeton, NJ: Princeton University Press.
Keynes, J.M. (1971–89), *The Collected Writings of John Maynard Keynes*, volumes I to XXX, London, published for the Royal Economic Society by Macmillan.
Khalil, E.L. (2000), 'Making Sense of Adam Smith's Invisible Hand: Beyond Pareto Optimality and Unintended Consequences'. *Journal of the History of Economic Thought*, **22**, (1), 49–63.
Kindleberger, C.P. (1978), *Manias, Panics and Crashes*. London: Macmillan.

Knight, F.H. (1921), *Risk, Uncertainty and Profit*. New York: Houghton, Mifflin.

Lehfeldt, R.A. (1912–13), 'The Rate of Interest on British and Foreign Investments'. *Journal of the Royal Statistical Society.*

Lewis, K.K. (1999), 'Trying to Explain Home Bias in Equities and Consumption'. *Journal of Economic Literature*, **XXXVII**, (2), 571–608.

MacCulloch, R.J. (1824), 'Standard of National Prosperity', *Edinburgh Review*, March, 19–20.

Marshall, A. (1879), 'The Theory of Foreign Trade and Other Portions of Economic Science Bearing on the Principle of Laissez Faire', in *The Early Economic Writings of Alfred Marshall, 1867–1890*, edited and introduced by J.K. Whitaker, vol. 2, London: Macmillan, 1975.

Marshall, A. (1923), *Money Credit and Commerce*. London: Macmillan.

Mill, J.S. (1848), *Principles of Political Economy*, reprinted in John M. Robson (ed.), *Collected Works of John Stuart Mill*, vols II–III, Toronto: University of Toronto Press, 1965.

Neal, L. (1990), *The Rise of Financial Capitalism,* Cambridge: Cambridge University Press.

Okina, K., M. Shirakawa and S. Shiratsuka (1999), 'Financial Market Globalization: Present and Future'. *Monetary and Economic Studies*, December, 1–40.

Persky, J. (1989), 'Adam Smith's Invisible Hand'. *Journal of Economic Perspectives*, **3**, (Fall), 195–201.

Ricardo, D. (1810), 'Notes on Bentham', reprinted in *The Works and Correspondence of David Ricardo*, edited by Piero Sraffa, vol. III, London: Cambridge University Press, 1951.

Ricardo, D. (1815–23), *Speeches and Evidence*, reprinted in *The Works and Correspondence of David Ricardo*, edited by Piero Sraffa, vol. V, London: Cambridge University Press, 1952.

Ricardo, D. (1817), *On the Principles of Political Economy and Taxation*, reprinted in *The Works and Correspondence of David Ricardo*, edited by Piero Sraffa, vol. I, London: Cambridge University Press, 1951.

Ricardo, D. (1819–21), *Letters*, now in *The Works and Correspondence of David Ricardo*, edited by Piero Sraffa, vol. VIII, London: Cambridge University Press, 1952.

Robbins, L. (1998), *A History of Economic Thought. The LSE Lectures*, edited by S.G. Medema and W.J. Samuels, Princeton, NJ: Princeton University Press.

Smith, A. (1776), *An Inquiry into the Nature and Causes of the Wealth of Nations*, reprinted in R.H. Campbell, A.S. Skinner and W.B. Todd (eds) (1976), *Glasgow Edition of the Works and Correspondence of Adam Smith,* vol. I, Oxford: Oxford University Press.

Strange, S. (1986), *Casino Capitalism*, Oxford: Blackwell.

Strange, S. (1998), *Mad Money. When Markets Outgrow Governments*, Ann Arbor: University of Michigan Press.

West, E.G. (1990), *Adam Smith and Modern Economics*, Aldershot: Edward Elgar.

2. Benign Neglect

Charles P. Kindleberger

In the field of political economy, political scientists and economists overlap to a considerable extent, but do not always see eye-to-eye. In discussion of politically-charged topics such as foreign exchange rates, both have something of a tendency to explain, rationalize and even defend national positions, often in an anthropomorphic way. Susan Strange and I were good friends; she invited me to talk in her seminar at LSE and to lecture at the Royal Institute of International Affairs (RIIA). She also sent me *Mad Money* (1998), which, with volume II of the RIIA *International Economic Relations of the Western World* (Shonfield 1976) plus detailed notes from an earlier reading of *Changing Fortunes: The World's Money and the Threat to American Leadership*, a discussion by Paul Volcker, onetime chairman of the Federal Reserve System, and Toyoo Gyohten, a leading financial expert in Japan (1992) are all the scholarly material at convenient hand for what follows.

It is assumed in political economy for the most part that countries are akin to individuals, taking decisions based on their own interests. Sometimes the interest is long run; altruistic action may be taken in the short. In the 1970s Susan Strange perceived a change in the attitude of the United States. It had had an 'extremely tender concern for Europe for 15 years after 1945', but afterward she detected 'Washington's frigid unconcern over the difficulties of money management of Germany, France, Britain and other European Countries' (1976, 266). American monetary policy, she believed, not only provided the material for hot money, but attracted or repelled it at its own convenience 'with scant regard for the disruptive effect this had on other countries' (Ibid.).

THREE PERIODS OF BENIGN NEGLECT

The adjectives 'tender', 'frigid', and 'scant' suggest that US neglect, if perhaps not malign, was hardly benign. The term 'benign neglect' was coined by New York Senator Patrick Moynihan, regarding the attitude white

Americans should take about blacks. It was well short of the Golden Rule of loving one's neighbor as oneself, but more friendly than a terse 'Mind your own business'. Its use in international monetary relations began with President Richard Nixon imposing import surcharges of 10 per cent in August 1971, followed by the Smithsonian Allied Agreement in December to a 10 per cent depreciation of the dollar. Agreement was required because it previously had been thought dollar depreciation was impossible: if the United States raised the price of gold, other countries would do so as well, leaving exchange rates unchanged. John Connally had been Secretary of the Treasury during the August and December 1971 episodes. He is reported as having said to the world: 'The dollar is our currency, but it's your problem'. Paul Volcker wrote 'Connally's cowboy tactics were secretly admired', (Volcker and Gyohten, 1992, 87). When he was followed in the position by George P. Shultz, neglect of the European allies became benign, rather than strongly self-centred. Shultz was benign, but, coming from the University of Chicago, believed in flexible exchange rates, Arthur Burns, the chairman of the Federal Reserve Board, on the other hand, favoured fixed rates (Volcker and Gyohten, 1992, 113). This lack of agreement may have contributed to neglect.

A second period of benign neglect occurred under President Ronald Reagan, after the inflation of the 1970s and the deflation of 1980–81. The United States had been concerned primarily with its monetary problems. These had been more or less overcome. But the higher interest rates produced by the stringent interest-rate policy attracted foreign capital, driving the dollar up, and threatening to produce balance-of-payments deficits and more deflation. It was time to take the dollar rate in hand. Secretary of the Treasury Baker, who had succeeded Donald Regan, negotiated the Plaza Agreement among the Allies, calling for coordinated intervention to stabilize currencies in the fall of 1985. Stability proved hard to achieve, and the dollar this time not only came down but continued to depreciate. In due course, the ministers of finance met again, this time at the Louvre in Paris in February 1987, agreeing to try to contain the fall. At the end of the decade there were boom and bust, especially in Japan, turning attention away from rates of exchange.

A third period of conscious benign neglect may be said to have started under Secretary of the Treasury Robert Rubin in the mid-1990s. This applied to Europe, but not to Mexico, the Far East, Brazil and Russia.

ON TERMINOLOGY

A number of distinctions may be helpful before proceeding further. There are, it seems to me, shades of difference between indifference and benign neglect, between hegemony and leadership, dominance and coercion. In *Mad Money*, Susan Strange wrote of 'American Indifference – what Americans like to call benign neglect' (1998, 67). I have tried to differentiate hegemony from leadership, the former with an implication of power, force, self-interest, the latter with persuasion and example. Most political scientists resist following this division, but Joseph S. Nye, Jr. comes close in separating 'hard' from 'soft-power,' with military overtones and persuasion, respectively (1990). Dominance, ascribed by François Perroux to the United States, was defined as a condition in which B has to respond to action taken by A, but A is unaffected by what happens in B, C, D and so on (Kindleberger 1961). In a prize-winning thesis in political science, Jonathan Kirschner claims that currency depreciation in a country, is often forced upon it by coercion of another country (1995). This goes quite far, as most currency depreciation, as I view them, are the result of mistakes in policy by the depreciating country, disasters such as war, bad harvests, earthquakes, or contagion spreading from another country which leads to herd behaviour of capital outflows.

There is, of course, the private good of a country, perhaps only staying out of trouble, and the international public good, the latter perhaps in the leading country's self-interest, but in the long run rather than the short. Provision of public goods, however, is often troubled by 'free riders', which benefit from the good but feel no obligation to contribute to its cost. When this occurs on a large scale, the country taking responsibility for the international system may grow weary under its disproportionate burden, and revert from the international to the national interest.

One or two other contrasts can be produced. Indifference is distinct from neglect, benign or malign, giving no attention to a problem rather than being aware of it with an attitude. Cooperation comes in two forms, active and passive, supporting and standing by without helping even though sympathetic. All these distinctions may be overdrawn, too subtle, and not particularly helpful, especially when they imply judgements, favourable or unfavourable.

NATIONAL BIASES IN ECONOMIC ANALYSIS

As already indicated, there is in this sort of discourse a tendency for analysts, including the author, to be less critical of their own country in these issues of international economic policy, and more critical of other countries. Moreover the perceptions of critics may read more national bias into a discussion than the writer or speaker feels or intended to convey. Economists claim to be detached and technical, but may be thought by political scientists to be chauvinistic and ignorant of the political implications of monetary or foreign exchange issues. Susan Strange tends to think of international economic problems as mostly political, and, to cite only one of many passages in this line, in borrowing a metaphor from military crises between countries, said that they in many ways more resemble monetary ones than do most diplomatic crises (1976, 313). Even *The Economist* viewed the paper, 'The Dollar and World Liquidity: a Minority View', as part of the 'new nationalism', whereas the authors thought they were making a clinically-detached point that the US balance-of-payments deficit on the liquidity definition, measured by the loss of gold and net short-term capital inflows, was a normal banking exchange of liquidity for foreign assets (and the good will generated by foreign aid) (Despres et al. 1966). Susan Strange has been critical of French moves in international finance, thinking in one instance it was holding back on cooperative aid to Britain (1976, 137–39; 1998, 149–53). A paper of mine can be interpreted as negative of French purposes in changing foreign exchange to gold, or threatening to do so, from Britain and Germany in the period from 1926 to 1936, and again *vis-à-vis* the dollar, 1960–70. It is principally addressed to the view that France, as a middle-range rather than Great Power, bit off more than it could chew (Kindleberger 1972). The United States was troubled by foreign central banks converting dollars into gold not only by France but by Japan, the United Kingdom, and the Belgians and Dutch, the last two on the assumption, Volcker wrote, that they were small and that their purchases would not affect the system (Volcker and Gyohten 1992, 55, 77, 83).

Strange's analysis of United States action is presented in fairly strong language: 'an iron fist in a velvet glove' (1976, 134); 'tyranny of the United States: unpleasant, painful, humiliating, but infinitely better than chaos' (ibid., 38); 'Japanese old-fashioned nationalists were fearful of American bullying and hypocrisy' (1998, 51); 'many Asians thought their troubles were engineered by Americans' (ibid., 110); 'the European Bank for Reconstruction and Development was under orders from the United States to make 60 percent of its loans to private borrowers' (ibid., 120); 'and the Japanese thought that the Bank of International Settlements Concordat on capital adequacy was a clever American ploy' (ibid., p. 161).

Anti-American sentiment of Andrew Shonfield was more strident. The United States wanted to avoid the blatant assertion of pure power, but under President Nixon tried to hustle its partners, dragged them, bullied, thrust and hustled them; fell into a mood of kicking over the table, leaving an empty chair (ibid., 1976, 48, 85–88). Shonfield further asserted that the Kennedy Round of the General Agreement on Tariffs and Trade was 'a simple exercise in United States hegemony', though in this he differed from the thought of Gerard and Victoria Curzon in the same volume; they wrote 'the Kennedy

Round constitutes the high-water mark in trade cooperation', and 'All the evidence suggests that the dominant country, oligopolistic model of trade relations does not account for postwar trade co-operation as well as the liberal-trade hypothesis. If any country lost, it was the United States' (Curzon and Curzon, 1976, 176, 200).

THE UNIT OF ANALYSIS PROBLEM: COUNTRIES AS NON-UNITARY ACTORS

Treating a country as a unit in international economics may miss key elements of domestic politics. John H. Williams ascribed Argentina's exchange policy in the last quarter of the nineteenth century to the response of the landowning oligarchy to international wheat prices: when the world price fell, depreciation of the peso held up the domestic price and kept growers' incomes steady while raising import prices of goods bought by urban peoples (Williams 1920). The British return to gold in 1925 was the work of the City of London; the Industrial north was not even consulted (Boyce 1987). President Herbert Hoover who was born in the Middle West and grew up in California, thought that the Eastern United States, the Federal Reserve Bank of New York, and especially Benjamin Strong, its governor, were 'a mental annex to Europe' (1962, vol. 3). A meeting of central bankers of England, France and Germany, along with the United States, was held in early July 1927 at the Long Island house of Ogden Mills, the US Secretary of the Treasury, presumably with the acceptance of the president. The New York Federal Reserve Bank lowered its discount rate subsequently to help Britain and France stabilize their currencies. Mills later showed little interest, was even described as apathetic, to Hoover's June 1931 call for a bold emphatic proposal for the United States to take the leadership in a moratorium on German reparations and Allied war debts. Mills said he needed the debt payment to balance the US budget. He seems to have been generally negative to international finance initiatives, as a year later he vetoed a suggestion of Herbert Feis, a State Department economic adviser, that the United States propose to the British a world economic conference (Morison, 1960, 347–50; Feis, 1966, 113).

There are occasions when central banks want to be left alone, especially if offers of help are regarded as an affront to their prestige. The Bank of England was irritated when the newly-founded Reichsbank offered to consult it about the handling of the sterling it has accumulated from the Franco-Prussian indemnity of 1871. It had no need for help from an upstart (Clapham, 1945, vol. 2, 294). It reacted similarly to a suggestion in France that the Bank of France had sold gold in London 1907 as a gesture of cooperation (Sayers, 1936, 104–13). On 21 September, 1931, Governor Clement Moret asked the Federal Reserve Bank of New York whether it would object if French dollars were converted into gold. Governor Harrison assured him it would not. The Bank of France had lost a considerable sum in forebearing from converting its sterling into gold in the summer of 1931, and the British government awarded him the title of a knight of the British Empire on that account. The French central bank withdrew gold steadily from New York through 1931 until it stopped of its own accord, giving the reason that it wanted to retain some earning assets to sustain its income (Federal Reserve Bank of New York files, discussed in Kindleberger, 1986, 164–65).

The Bank of International Settlements had been established under the Owen Young Plan of 1930 to transfer reparations from Germany to the European allies. After the moratorium of June 1931, it was transformed into a club for central bankers to meet monthly and exchange information, views and on occasion develop devices for cooperation. The Federal Reserve System first sent observers, then joined the board, and in 1960, under the leadership of Charles Coombs, the New York Federal Reserve's vice-president in charge of foreign exchange, devised what developed into a system of central bank swap lines. Starting in 1962, the Bank of France and the Federal Reserve Bank of New York credited each other with $50 million of local currency. The pair were quickly joined by the Dutch, Belgian and Canadian central banks, and then the Swiss National Bank. By October 1963, the network covered 11 central banks, with the equivalent of $2 billion available as credit. Amounts rose to $4.5 billion in September 1966, $9 billion in March 1968, and after the break-up of the Bretton Woods system and the floating of the dollar, to $18 billion by July 1973 (Coombs 1976). In time of need, the country in trouble would draw on its lines of credit for six months and either repay or fund them when the term was up. As one crisis followed another, Coombs's response was to persuade the other central banks to enlarge the swap lines.

The Bretton Woods system had been extended earlier in 1960 by the General Agreements to Borrow in which the 10 leading governments pledged $6 billion on top of $14.4 billion of IMF quotas, to be used to offset undesirable flows of short-term capital. It was the inadequacy of the amount that led to the swap lines. In the course of subsequent operations, the Bank of France abstained from a package to help the British organize a squeeze against bears selling sterling in September 1965, 'a shocking repudiation of central bank free-masonry'. The British nonetheless received the credit they wanted. Later, in June 1966, the French again stood aside, from the swap network, but arranged a separate bilateral central bank credit with conditions (Strange 1976, 136).

BENIGN NEGLECT 1971–PRESENT

Andrew Shonfield has written that a country running a reserve currency
almost of necessity followed policies different from those that apply to other
countries (1976, I, 37). Many economists have held that no country can
succeed long in maintaining a stable exchange rate, free movement
internationally of capital and an independent monetary policy (in some
versions free trade is added). In an earlier work, I listed five functions which
a country which assumed responsibility for leading the world economy
should discharge:

1. maintaining a relatively open market for distress goods;
2. providing counter-cyclical, or at least stable, long-term lending;
3. policing a relatively stable system of exchange rates;
4. ensuring the coordination of macro-economic policies;
5. acting as a lender of last resort in financial crises (1986, 289).

For this discussion, trade and the lender-of-last-resort functions can be
neglected, the latter of which is being taken over by the International
Monetary Fund, dominated in some views, by the United States Treasury.

   The period of neglect of the chapter's interest starts with the serious
mistake in monetary policy made by the Federal Reserve System in 1970 and
1971 under the Board chairmanship of Arthur Burns. In order to stimulate the
American economy and help assure the re-election of Richard Nixon as
president, the System started to lower interest rates in the United States. The
mistake was to adopt this policy at a time when the Bundesbank in the
Federal Republic of Germany was tightening interest rates to fend off
inflation, a subject on which it was paranoid after the hyperinflations after
World Wars I and II. The American and German money markets were
connected through the Euro-dollar market which had evolved in the 1960s,
and was located primarily in London. Lower interest rates in New York
precipitated a flow of funds to London, lowering rates there. Corporations in
Germany, at first multinational and then German, borrowed Euro-dollars to
pay off deutschmark debt, selling the Euro-dollars to the Bundesbank, which
redeposited them in the Euro-market in London, thus letting loose the money
multiplier. The world money stock soared. Conversions of dollars to gold
increased. Worried more about the capital account in the United States
balance of payments than trade, the Nixon administration in August 1971,
believing that it could not depreciate the dollar since other countries would
match an increase in the gold price, imposed a 10 per cent surcharge on
imports and adopted price controls. The events of August were followed in
December 1971 by at agreement at the Smithsonian Institution in
Washington, where depreciation of the dollar by 10 per cent replaced the

import surcharge. It failed to stabilize the dollar, and United States administration gave up the Smithsonian rate. This ultimately led Germany to float the deutschmark against the dollar in 1973, inaugurating the first stage of 'benign neglect'. There is, to be sure, a question whether the neglect begun with floating was truly benign or rather one of indifference, as Susan Strange implied. In her view, markets had taken power away from governments (including central banks), leaving them, apart from a few like the German, unwilling any longer to act collectively, although European exchange rates were still vulnerable to US policies (Strange 1998, 67).

The Shonfield admission that the policies of the reserve currency, or perhaps those of a leading country taking responsibility for the system differ from those of others, suggests that the rule that no country can maintain fixed exchange rates, free capital movement, and independent monetary policy should be treated differently by the leader on the one hand and by followers on the other. For the leader stable macro-economic policy and free capital movement may dominate, with the exchange rate determined by followers accepted passively. For the followers, the power to determine independent monetary policies tend to be undermined, being dominated by the leading country, provided its macro-economic policies are reasonably stable. This division of function is the theoretical justification for the leading reserve currency to neglect its exchange rate. For a limited example, Canada may worry what the Canadian dollar-US dollar exchange rate is, and some industries in the United States may be concerned, but the United States as a whole tends not to be.

This much said, the United States did badly in 1970 and 1971, maintaining reasonable macro-economic policies, as noted above. With dollars flooding abroad and world inflation spurting in the 1970s, the Federal Reserve under the chairmanship of Paul Volcker switched policies at the end of the decade, raising interest rates sharply. The flow of short-term capital reversed direction, and, with floating, pushed the dollar so high that it could no longer be unattended. Susan Strange quotes an unpublished dissertation of 1986 at the European University Institute in Florence by H. Feddersen to the effect that the United States was indifferent to the dollar-DM exchange rate, so concerned it was with domestic macro-economic policy, but changed its mind when the dollar markedly appreciated and later declined (1998, 67).

The push of the United States first in 1985 at the Plaza Hotel in New York to urge foreign central banking intervention to lower the dollar rate, and then in February 1987 at the Louvre in Paris to halt its depreciation, brought a stop to benign neglect of the US exchange rate.

Rapid recovery following the New York stock-market crash of Black Monday, 19 October 1987, helped by lender-of-last resort action by the Federal Reserve Bank of New York, proved reassuring for the rest of the

1980s. The 1990s started off badly with the collapse of a stock-market and real-estate bubble in Japan, partly stimulated – the bubble not the collapse – by US pressure on Japanese authorities and others to lower interest rates to assist in world recovery (Volcker and Gyohten, 1992, 271–75). Fallout from Japan produced a mild slowdown in the United States, but by 1994 attention turned to Mexico with another financial crisis following one in 1982. This was contained by infusion of liquidity amounting to the staggering sum of $50 billion, from Bretton Woods institutions, the Inter-American Development Bank, central banks and the US Stabilization Fund. European exchange rates were ignored by official institutions, despite a hedge-fund attack on the pound sterling and the Italian lira in 1992 and 1993. United States fiscal policy was helped by the collapse of the Soviet Union which made possible a decline in defence spending. Unemployment fell to new lows, the rate of price increases declined to tolerable levels, technical progress increased sharply and consumer spending kept climbing to sustain increases in output.

There were, however, some signs of danger. Stock-market and real-estate prices kept rising, most notably in high-tech industry areas. Consumer savings declined to vanishing point as credit-card debt and home-equity loans (second mortgages) climbed to new levels. Consumer spending and sluggish incomes abroad raised imports more than exports and increased the trade deficit to almost $300 billion in 1999. While wages rose only slowly, labour shortages in many places worried authorities that a sharp rise in wages and prices might lie ahead. Financial crises in Asia 1997, in Brazil and Russia in 1998, and the collapse of the Long-Term Capital Management hedge fund in September 1998 were overcome more rapidly than initially anticipated, but still left a residue of anxiety. Optimists believed that the 'New Era' in information technology and successful handling of monetary policy by the Federal Reserve System held the promise of sustained stability and growth. A considerable number of analysts, however, saw the potential for shocks to the system that might burst the bubbles in asset prices, and lead to a process of debt deflation as in the 1930s. More and more, analysts and forecasters in the United States focused attention on domestic events and prospects, on the whole giving little attention to economic happenings abroad.

One more particular subject in foreign exchange deserves the tag of American benign neglect, the course of the euro. This had its start on 1 January 1999, after the decision at Maastricht. Strongly influenced by the sturdy deutschmark, the first quotation for the new currency were on the order of 110 to the dollar of 100 cents. Many economic analysts expected the euro to appreciate as countries outside the European Union moved working balances into euros from dollars. There was a different view, however, that with the integration of European capital markets, the outside countries might borrow there even for purchases made with dollars, holding down the rise of the euro and even depressing it somewhat (McCauley, 1997). This in fact took place, and by early 2000 the euro had declined from 110 to 100, and in a few days, below 90.

Appreciation of the dollar this time did not, as in the first half of the 1980s produce a reaction in Washington. Lawrence Summers, who succeeded Robert Rubin as Secretary of the Treasury, said he welcomed dollar strength, without implying any particular satisfaction or regret in the change.

Opinion among American analysts on the success of the European Monetary Union and the euro was divided, as it was in Britain. In the United States most concern was felt about whether successful integration could be achieved without a substantial common budget with an implied automatic stabilizing mechanism responding to regional shocks in the system. The discussion was less intense than in the United Kingdom with its need to decide in the future whether or not to join the pound to the euro. Prime Minister Tony Blair is committed to a referendum on the question after the next election. As Susan Strange has suggested, however, the decision may well be made by markets rather than governments, another Darwinian outcome like the Euro-dollar market and the still evolving international lender-of-last-resort function, not planned, but one which like Topsy in *Uncle Tom's Cabin*, just grew.

A PARALLEL FROM INTERNATIONAL TRADE

While Susan Strange's interest in benign neglect, or as she saw it, indifference, was focused on exchange rates and capital flows, it is possible to find a loose parallel in tariff policies, going back well to the beginning of the nineteenth century, that is, whether or not to demand reciprocal reductions abroad for one's own reductions, and to retaliate for tariff increases applied by trading partners abroad. Robert Axelrod, a political scientist, claims that the optimal strategy in game theory is to retaliate, but this applies to two-person repeated games in which the purpose is to teach the other player to co-operate (1984). It seems somewhat out of character that Adam Smith in *The Theory of Moral Sentiments*, produced the same sentiment, writing 'As every man doeth, so it shall be done to him, and retaliation seems to be the great law which is dictated to us by nature' (1808, I, 191). But it is hard to find a common thread of reciprocity or unilateral tariff action with indifference to the response of others in tariff history.

The era of tariff reductions in the nineteenth century begins with unilateral reductions on the part of Great Britain, following the imposition of high tariffs on grain in the 1820s when prices fell sharply after the Napoleonic wars. William Huskisson was a free trader at the time, and lowered certain tariffs such as that on French silk without demanding the reciprocity that had been a feature of the Treaty of Vergennes (Eden) of 1786. A book by Henry Parnell on tariff reductions was entitled *Financial Reform* (1830) and in the early 1840s the British government abolished duties on a long list of imports on which the small value of duties collected was barely worth the trouble of collecting. The movements occurred after the Reform Bill of 1832 which shifted political power from landed gentry with agricultural interests to urban dwellers. The major movement came in 1846 with the repeal of the Corn Laws, followed by that of the timber duties and the Navigation Acts. The unilateral nature of these actions had perhaps two roots: (1), the belief of David Hume of the eighteenth century that imports generated exports; and (2), a view especially of John Bowring and others at the Board of Trade that freeing up imports from the Continent would slow down its industrialization in competition with the Industrial Revolution of Great Britain. This notion has been called 'free-trade imperialism', (Gallagher and Robinson 1953; Semmel 1970), a term which a few commentators in developing countries have applied to United States efforts to lower tariffs and restrictions abroad, in goods and services, especially in the Uruguay Round.

The repeal movement of the late 1840s in Britain on a unilateral basis was followed by the Anglo-French (Cobden-Chevalier) treaty of 1860, objected to on the French side by industry but imposed by Louis Napoleon III under the influence of free-trader Michel Chevalier. Tariff reductions by other treaties went on in Europe until 1879, when Otto Bismarck of Prussia imposed the so-called tariff of 'rye and iron', advocated by Prussian agriculture and Ruhr steel, and leading to a wave of tariffs on the Continent. The British did not retaliate to this, nor to the American McKinley tariff of 1890 on such import items as Welsh tinplate responding to the rapidly-expanding canning industry. Proposals for retaliation were made by Austin Chamberlain, along lines of Empire preference, but lacked success. British free-trade ideology dominated the country until the depression beginning in 1929.

The United States went its own way in tariff making, up under McKinley, down under Wilson (the Underwood), without interest in reciprocity until after the violent retaliation of foreign countries, Canada, Spain, Switzerland and then the British Commonwealth in the Ottawa Agreement of 1932, unleashed by the Hawley-Smoot tariff under President Hoover (Jones 1934). In the depression, free-traders led by Cordell Hull, Secretary of State, struggled with import competing agricultural interests, until the former won, producing the Reciprocal Trade Agreement Act of 1934. En route, the British imposed a reciprocal trade and payments agreement on Argentina in the Roca-Runciman treaty of 1933, exploiting its monopoly position in Argentine exports. The United States was in the same position *vis-à-vis* Brazil in coffee, but ignored the opportunity to capitalize on it (de Paiva Abreu, 1984). Nor did the United States or any other developed country retaliate to the price increases in oil of 1973 and 1979, engineered by the Organization of Petroleum Exporting Countries, (largely at that time from the Middle East), or the countries of the New International Economic Order (NIEO), which threatened to raise the prices of other primary products such as bauxite, rubber and tin. The relaxed attitude may have been induced by fears that retaliation would not succeed in keeping prices from rising, from a (realistic) calculation that monopoly action would fail to work, but more probably because the developed countries discriminated in policy between developed and developing countries, and in relevant conditions.

Susan Strange noted that in the immediate circumstances following World War II, the United States pushed vigorously for European recipients of aid to open their markets to one another, preached freer trade and non-discrimination in general, but did not object to recipients of US aid in the initial stages and under the European Recovery Program (Marshall Plan) maintaining quotas on non-vital American exports (1976). As the Golden Age of the quarter-century after 1945 came to an end, this relaxed attitude changed.

The United States pushed hard to successive rounds of tariff reduction on a reciprocal basis under the General Agreement on Tariffs and Trade, an executive agreement adopted by the United States after the failure of the Congress to accept the International Trade Organization negotiated at Havana in 1948 under American auspices. When this was transformed into the World Trade Organization, provision was made for countries to retaliate when another state raised tariffs or imposed other restrictions on their exports. The provision was presumably agreed in order to limit these restrictions. As it worked out, however, the United States applied retaliatory restrictions against other developed countries, especially in luxury products, in its own interest, and in the case of European discrimination against Central American bananas, in support of its Latin American friends.

CONCLUSION

Circumstances alter cases. It is hard to derive a set of valid generalizations from the foregoing, whether countries always act in their national interest, short or long-term; on behalf of domestic interests such as capital, labour, landowners, or multinational corporations; or discriminate, with one rule for their peers and another for the remainder. Is the pressure for free or freer trade, altruistic, free-trade imperialism, or some shifting combination of the two, with the same question to be asked about pressuring developing countries to raise the incomes of their wage-earners, and take greater care of the environment? Are international economic issues of trade and capital flows basically political rather than technical questions of optimization, as economists think they are, and from which political scientists dissent?

I am fond quoting an aphorism attributed to Frank Knight, the distinguished University of Chicago economist, but for which I have not found a citation: 'The true Christian who loves his neighbor as himself, and the economic man who maximizes his personal advantage are alike in that neither has any friends.' Countries like people are not always consistent, nor do they operate uniformly in the national public interest, as opposed occasionally – perhaps often and for an extended period – on behalf of powerful domestic forces. Moreover, they make mistakes from time to time. I do not mind if Susan Strange, like most of us, occasionally changes her point of view, but I am not readily willing to concede that international monetary (and even trade) questions rest at basis on politics, rather than on economics, or perhaps better, political economy.

ADDENDUM

After finishing writing this chapter, I found in the *Economic History Review*, for February 2000 (vol. LIII, no. 1, p. 164) in the 'Review of Periodical Literature' by Roger Middleton, the expression 'the dominant voice in this issue of the European Customs Union was that of 'traditional' British benevolent non-participation,' a concept not far from benign neglect.

REFERENCES

Axelrod, Robert (1984), *The Evolution of Cooperation*, New York: Basic Books.
Boyce, Robert W.D. (1987), *British Capitalism at the Crossroads 1919–1932: A Study in Politics, Economics, and International Relations*, Cambridge: Cambridge University Press.
Clapham, Sir John (1945), *The Bank of England: A History*, 2 vols, Cambridge: Cambridge University Press.
Coombs, Charles A. (1976), *The Arena of International Finance*, New York: Wiley-Interscience.
Curzon, Gerard and Victoria Curzon (1976), 'The Management of Trade Relations in GATT,' in Andrew Shonfield (ed.), *International Economic Relations of the Western World, 1959–1971*, London: Oxford University Press, vol. 2, pp.145–280.
de Paiva Abreu (1984), 'Argentina and Brazil during the 1930s: the Impact of British and American International Economic Policies,' in Rosemary Thorp (ed.), *Latin American in the 1930s: The Periphery in World Crisis*, London: Macmillan, pp.144–82.

Despres, Emile, C.P. Kindleberger and W.S. Salant (1966), 'The Dollar and World Liquidity: A Minority View,' *The Economist*, vol. 218, no. 6389, 5 February.

Feddersen, H. (1986), 'The Management of Floating Exchange Rates: The Case of the D-Mark-Dollar Rate, 1973–1983,' unpublished PhD dissertation, European University Institute, Florence, Italy.

Feis, Herbert (1966), *1933: Characters in Crisis*, Boston: Little, Brown.

Gallagher, John and Ronald Robinson (1953), 'The Imperialism of Free Trade', *Economic History Review*, vol. 6, no. l, pp. 1–15.

Hoover, Herbert (1952), *The Memoirs of Herbert Hoover*, vol. 3, *The Great Depression, 1929–1941*, New York: Macmillan.

Jones, Joseph M. (1934), *Tariff Retaliation: Repercussions of the Hawley-Smoot Bill*, Philadelphia: University of Pennsylvania Press.

Kindleberger, C.P. (1961), 'La fin du rôle dominant des Etats-Unis et l'avenir d'un politique économique mondiale,' *Cahiers de l'Institut des Sciences Economiques Appliquées*, 113 (May), pp. 91–105.

Kindleberger, C.P. (1972), 'The International Monetary Politics of a Near-Great Power: two French Episodes, 1926–1935, and 1960–1970,' *Economic Notes* I, 2–3, pp. 30–44.

Kindleberger, C.P. (1981), 'Dominance and Leadership in the International Economy: Exploitation, Public Goods, and Free Rides,' *International Studies Quarterly*, vol. 25, no. 2, pp. 242–54.

Kindleberger, C.P. (1986), *The World in Depression, 1929–1939*, 2nd edn, Berkeley: University of California Press.

Kirschner, Jonathan (1995), *Currency and Coercion*, Princeton, NJ: Princeton University Press.

McCauley, Robert N. (1997), 'The Euro and the Dollar,' *Essays in International Finance*, 205 (November), Princeton, NJ: International Finance Section.

Morison, Elting E. (1960), Turmoil and Tradition: A Study of the Life and Times of Henry Stimson, Boston: Houghton Mifflin.

Nye, Joseph S. Jr. (1990), *Bound to Lead: The Changing Nature of American Power*, New York: Basic Books.

Parnell, Henry (1830), *Financial Reform*.

Sayers, R.S. (1936), *Bank of England Operations, 1890–1914*, London: P.S. King.

Semmel, Bernard (1970), The Rise of Free Trade and Imperialism: Classical Political Economy, The Empire of Free Trade and Imperialism, 1750–1850, Cambridge: Cambridge University Press.

Shonfield, Andrew (ed.) (1976), *International Economic Relations of the Western World, 1959–1971*, 2 vols, London: Oxford University Press.

Smith, Adam (1808), *The Theory of Moral Sentiments: or an Essay Toward an Analysis of the Principles by which Men Naturally Judge Concerning the Conduct and Character, First of their Neighbors, and afterwards of Themselves*, 11th edn, Edinburgh: Bell and Bradfute.

Strange, Susan (1976), 'International Monetary Relations,' in A. Shonfield, (ed.), *International Economic Relations in the Western World, 1959–1971*, vol. 2, London: Oxford University Press.

Strange, Susan (1998), *Mad Money*, Manchester: Manchester University Press.

Volcker, Paul A. and Toyoo Gyohten (1992), *Changing Fortunes: The World's Money and the Threat to American Leadership*, New York: Times Books.

Williams, John H. (1920), *Argentine International Trade under Inconvertible Paper Money, 1880–1900*, Cambridge, MA: Harvard University Press.

3. Musings on the World Political Economy of the Future: A Plural Global System?

David Calleo

CASINO CHAOS?

Susan Strange would doubtless be amused to hear herself called a Romantic. But like the great nineteenth century Romantic observers of the human condition, she combined two opposite but complementary traits. She was acutely sensitive to the kaleidoscopic particulars of social, political and economic life. She loved, for example, to track the peregrinations of the world's footloose firms, entrepreneurs and speculators. As a result, she often sensed critical changes before many other academic analysts. But like the best Romantics, she also had a strong strategic instinct, a sense for how particulars were mysteriously connected and heading somewhere. She thus perceived large issues evolving through the swirling details of everyday events. In particular, she noted, early on, the great explosion of volatile money that transformed global markets and national economies in the latter part of the twentieth century. And she had strong sense of the political and economic dangers lying in wait. She saw highly charged money, coursing around the world economy, like sugar in the veins of a diabetic – a powerfully destructive force. She never forgot that volatile money, which fuels growth, can also tear apart economies, states and societies. With *Casino Capitalism*, this image of excess money out of control became her trademark.

While she was adumbrating the dangers of the world's glut of liquid capital, she also sensed how the world economy had adapted to it. Hedging, in all its multifarious forms, became a way not only for operators to profit hugely, but provided security to actors in the real economy. Speculation was thereby converted into a means for lowering and sharing risk – for shoring up the system rather than wrecking it.

Notwithstanding all this systemic 'cunning of reason' at work, the global financial edifice has seemed more and more ramshackle. For all the frantic ingenuity of international finance, the prospect of a 'meltdown' has been haunting markets everywhere as the new century begins. Susan, like many other analysts, was inclined to read the successive financial shocks of the 1990s as a rolling breakdown of the system as a whole – with temporary recoveries followed by renewed crises. The years since Susan's death have, for many people, only reinforced this view. By the turn of the century, the manic flood of world money was flowing into equity markets, those of the US in particular, where the ratio of prices to earnings reached levels manifestly unsustainable by historical standards. Now, in late 2001, with shares falling and the economy slowing, and sympathetic movements in Europe and Japan, there is widespread fear of a new global crisis emanating from America.

Fear of a breakdown is nothing new. It has been characteristic of several periods during the postwar decades. The late 1960s and early 1970s, for example, saw the gradual disintegration of the Bretton Woods international monetary arrangements, accompanied by widespread inflation and the first oil shock. The late 1970s and early 1980s saw renewed inflation, oil shocks and currency speculation, with a very large American fiscal deficit, a superheated dollar and various 'debt crises' in Latin America, including a major crisis in Mexico. The late 1980s saw a sharp devaluation of the dollar followed by a crisis in Japan, as that country's bloated stock and real estate markets imploded. A financial crisis and general recession also occurred in Europe, as the European Monetary System of the day began to fall to pieces. Then came another Mexican financial crisis, one that spread to Brazil. Meanwhile a major Asian crisis erupted in 1997, followed by a severe collapse of the Russian rouble.

In all these instances, however, the global system rallied to contain its problems. And even if the fallout was often prolonged and severe for the regions and institutions affected, the worst was nevertheless avoided and the system recovered its momentum. The global economy as a whole went forward to still greater general prosperity. Nothing, of course, guarantees that the future will be like the past in this respect. Nevertheless, a long-standing pattern – stretching over several decades – suggests that the postwar system has impressive capabilities for managing its crises and for recuperating from them.

BENEVOLENT HEGEMONY

The capacity for fixing crises has been inseparable from the leading role of the United States. Charles Kindleberger has long been arguing forcefully that

a liberal world political economy needs a hegemonic power to manage it.[1]
Certainly, the postwar global political economy has been a hegemonic system
from its inception. America's heavy foreign investment and consumption of
foreign products have been powerful accelerators for growth around the
world. And the US has been the principal stabilizer in emergencies – the
world's lender and buyer of last resort. The US has been able to finance its
high consumption and investment over the years thanks, not least, to the
international role of the dollar, a role that has carried with it the 'exorbitant
privilege' of creating global money at will. America's global monetary
hegemony, because it is so expansive, has itself been a motor for postwar
growth, as well as a fertile source of inflation.

The postwar American contribution, of course, goes well beyond the
economic sphere. The US has also been the global system's principal
provider of military security. It has sustained the nuclear and conventional
deterrence needed to keep a peaceful strategic balance among the major
powers. During the Cold War, the US also assumed, through its alliances,
primary responsibility for regional security in Europe, the Middle East, and
East Asia. In short, America's exorbitant privilege in creating money was
matched by its exorbitant responsibility for making the world system work.

All in all, the Cold War system functioned very well as a hegemonic Pax
Americana. By 1991, the US was able to see off its geopolitical and
ideological rival of the Cold War – the 'Marxist' USSR. The Soviet collapse
not only brought a huge remaining piece of the globe into the capitalist world
political economy, but also seemed to reaffirm the hegemonic or 'unipolar'
character of that global system. America's primacy in the 1990s was further
reinforced by a remarkable period of its own national growth. Since the US
had borne the greatest share of Western military burdens during the Cold
War, it was able to reap the benefits of a very large 'peace dividend'
thereafter, thanks to rapid and radical cuts in military spending that began in
the first Bush administration. These, together with some creative financing
of American debt during the Clinton administration, gradually ended
America's hitherto huge fiscal deficit.[2] A major period of technological
innovation, coupled with an investment boom in fashionable new technology,
was accompanied by a remarkable rise in American productivity.[3] The
collapse of the Soviet Union thus coincided with a rejuvenation of the United
States itself. The hegemonic role of the Americans seemed doubly ratified.

TROUBLES AHEAD? FINANCING AMERICA'S FOREIGN DEFICIT

Assuming reasonable competence in managing the occasional crises of exuberant capitalism, why should so successful a global system ever end? Why are Susan's old fears so widely shared? Many people worry that the system's fundamentals are unsound. Probably the most worrisome symptom is America's heavy external deficit. A record current account deficit has continued to grow, despite the apparent success of the American economy in the 1990s – with low inflation, fiscal balance and record exports. But if a large and persistent external deficit is a symptom of disease, the US has been ill for a long time. Arguably, the US has run an external deficit of one sort or another since the end of World War II. Indisputably, it has had a trade deficit since the 1970s and regular current-account deficit since the 1980s.[4] In other words, the US has long been consuming and investing more than it produces.

The US has never had great trouble financing its deficits. When one formula was exhausted, another one was quickly found.[5] Sometimes, as in the 1960s, the US simply created money and exported it. At other times, as in the 1980s, the US borrowed back the dollars it had exported. Recently, America's deficit has been financed by a large inflow of private foreign capital, heavily European, flowing into a booming stock market. This inflow has taken place despite Europe's own relatively modest boom, and the apparently successful launching of the euro. Indeed the euro's subsequent chronic weakness and the dollar's remarkable strength have been clearly linked to Europe's outflow of capital to America. The recent volatile decline of American stock markets suggests, however, that this particular financing formula may be reaching its term. But why should it prove any more difficult for the US to come up with a quick and easy new source of foreign financing than previously? After so many decades, why should the external deficit now be a danger to American prosperity, or to the stability of the global economy?

The answer depends on the potential effects of the euro. The euro will provide large holders of international capital with an alternative reserve and transactions currency. They will no longer be compelled to hold most of their liquid wealth in dollars. To attract foreign investors to dollars, the US will be forced to keep its interest rates competitive. All else being equal, an ever-rising external debt will cost more and more to service. Higher real interest rates are the likely consequence and they will not be good for America's growth, nor for its stock market, particularly one that is already ailing. Insofar as high rates push up the dollar, that will not be good for America's trade deficit either. Trade problems may be expected to grow more difficult.[6]

In the Cold War years, the US, as the West's military protector, could usually assure the financing of its various deficits merely by raising the issue of Europe's reluctant 'burden sharing'. Europe had no great desire to manage its own defence against the Soviet Union. Today's situation is different and seems unlikely to be reversed by the 'war on terrorism'. Without the Soviet threat, Europeans are increasingly inclined to manage their security more independently. Hence the European Union's drive for Common Foreign and Security Policy (CFSP), a European Security and Defence Identity in NATO (ESDI) and the European Security and Defence Policy (ESDP) – accompanied and reinforced by significant cross-country mergers in European defence industries.[7] In short, geopolitics no longer so strongly reinforces America's old monetary hegemony. Thus, given the euro, finding cheap financing for the habitual American deficit may grow more and more problematic.

The problem is not the euro, of course, but the deficit. In the 1980s and early 1990s, America's big current-account deficit could be blamed on its 'twin', the very large fiscal deficit, which could, in turn, be blamed on the country's relatively heavy military spending. A large government deficit, together with habitually low private saving, filled the standard macroeconomic explanation for a current account deficit: The US was 'absorbing' – consuming and investing – more than it produced. The difference came from other economies. Hence the large external deficit.[8]

With the 'peace dividend', America's giant fiscal deficit of the 1980s gradually disappeared. Under the Clinton administration, the federal government began running a fiscal surplus, in other words, saving rather than 'dissaving'. Nevertheless, the external deficit kept on growing. Whatever the government saved, the private economy absorbed still more.[9] Even though American exports reached new highs, American imports increased even faster. America's huge current account deficits accelerated into the new century. To cut that deficit would presumably require reducing consumption, thus lowering the standard of living; or it would require reducing investment, thus lowering growth. Not surprisingly, Americans have not been eager to do either.[10]

THE ASIAN PROBLEM

Reluctance to see America's big external deficit end is by no means limited to the Americans themselves. It has been a welcome bonanza to exporters all around the rest of the world. This seems particularly true for Asian economies, China included. For decades, big trade deficits with Asia have been a principal component of America's overall external deficit.[11]

America's role as absorber of Asia's exports is so great that during the region's crisis of the 1990s, the U.S. was frequently described, indeed described itself officially, as Asia's buyer of last resort.[12] Today's fears of global instability are very much bound up with memories of that Asian currency crisis.[13] Its apparent causes seem ominous portents for the future of the global economy. More specifically, they reveal why it may be difficult and perhaps dangerous for the US to reduce its current-account deficit sharply.

Initially, postwar Asia's high rate of investment and growth were powered primarily by ample domestic savings and healthy trade surpluses. By the 1990s, with the progressive elimination of capital controls, there were also large inflows of foreign capital – much of it short-term or for portfolio investment.[14] Most Asian currencies were tied to the dollar, a logical link given the importance of the American market for their exports. As the dollar went up sharply in 1997, many Asian currencies began to have trouble sustaining their old exchange rates. Speculators and investors, anticipating devaluations, began withdrawing their capital. Banks, long accustomed to ample foreign inflows, and therefore to borrowing short and lending long, suddenly found themselves in serious trouble. Habitual banking practices, highly successful for decades, suddenly became unsound. 'Asian values' – loyalty to old clients and friends, business conducted on the basis of connections and reputation, high leveraging of debt in general – characteristics often lauded as the source of Asian capitalism's apparent efficiency and rapid growth – suddenly appeared corrupt and dysfunctional. As credit tightened and competitive conditions deteriorated, firms found themselves abruptly deprived of normal credit lines. Sound businesses were swept aside along with weak ones. In many countries, huge conglomerates fell to pieces and were easy prey for foreign buyers. The region's various real estate and stock market bubbles began to burst. After a series of severe currency and financial crises, a deep recession followed in most of the region.

Doubtless, the sharply rising dollar proved a trigger for the crisis. But the dollar had risen even more sharply before – notably in the 1980s during America's experiment with Reaganomics – without anything like the same damaging consequences for Asia's booming economies.[15] It was natural to blame the crisis on the lack of professional standards in Asian banking systems, or on the illiberal and corrupt nature of Asian business practices generally. But behind the collapse of the banks was a basic change in the competitive climate. For Asia, one obvious difference between the early 1980s and the late 1990s was the greatly increased significance of Chinese trade. Chinese exports as a proportion of all exports for East Asia and the Pacific increased from 15.9 per cent in 1980 to 25.4 per cent in 1990, and reached a level of 33.6 per cent in 1998.[16]

China's conversion into a highly competitive world trading power constituted a major change in the global economic and political system. In constant dollars, China's exports nearly quadrupled from 1978 to 1990, and more than doubled from 1990 to 1995. Of these exports, 3.2 per cent went to the US in 1978 and 17.7 per cent in 1996.[17] As the new China emerged, the basic competitive position of the smaller East Asian economies tended to deteriorate.[18] World markets had begun to experience a strong deflationary trend.[19] Non-Chinese export industries in Asia began to look vulnerable. Under these circumstances, the shock of a sharp dollar appreciation in the later 1990s was enough to restrict the hitherto abundant capital flows to the smaller and more developed Asian economies.

In soothing the region's currency crisis, the US was not only Asia's lender of last resort – its hegemonic financier – but also its buyer of last resort. America's trade deficit, while still growing with Japan and the various Asian 'tigers', as well as with Europe, increased stunningly with China. From 1995 to 2000, the American bilateral deficit with China jumped from $37 billion to $90 billion – a sum higher than America's long-standing deficit with Japan in 2000 ($85 billion), and one and a half times its deficit with the EU ($59 billion) (see Table 3.1). Selling Asia's exports, swollen by China's explosive production, grew ever more dependent on the American market, that is to say on the American trade deficit.

Table 3.1: US Bilateral Trade Balance with Principal Partners
(millions of US dollars)

	China	Japan	EU	NAFTA
1994	-32 075	-68 989	-16 254	-17 217
1995	-36 772	-62 897	-13 257	-38 724
1996	-42 431	-50 427	-19 947	-44 512
1997	-53 027	-58 593	-21 222	-37 105
1998	-60 851	-67 203	-32 288	-40 964
1999	-73 537	-76 276	-47 720	-58 989
2000	-90 251	- 84 982	-58 702	- 80 904

Source: International Monetary Fund *Direction of Trade Statistics Yearbook 2001*, pp. 476–478.

Table 3.2: Various Asian Trade Balances/(Total Exports) (millions of US dollars)

	China (Mainland)	Malaysia	South Korea	Indonesia	Singapore	Thailand
1994	5 160	-806	-6 142	8 069	-5 731	-8 811
	(120 865)	(58 749)	(96 389)	(40 054)	(96 911)	(45 583)
1995	16 792	-3 896	-9 764	4 799	-6 207	-16 491
	(148 955)	(73 724)	(125 588)	(45 428)	(118 187)	(57 201)
1996	12 216	-227	-19 668	6 971	-6 204	-17 593
	(151 165)	(78 214)	(130 994)	(49 873)	(125 125)	(55 743)
1997	40 754	-138	-8 569	11 759	-7 265	-5 244
	(182 917)	(78 909)	(136 354)	(53 439)	(125 326)	(57 560)
1998	43 359	15 151	39 333	21 506	8 280	11 381
	(183 744)	(73 470)	(132 703)	(48 843)	(109 886)	(54 489)
1999	29 213	19 059	23 907	24 652	3 659	8 590
	(194 931)	(84 550)	(143 647)	(48 652)	(114 730)	(61 797)
2000	24 099	15 958	11 347	28 591	3 302	8 245
	(249 195)	(98 153)	(171 826)	(62 102)	(137 932)	(65 160)

Note: As the table clearly shows, China was the only of these developing East Asian economies to register a consistent increase in exports during the period 1994 to 2000. With the exception of Indonesia, China was also the only economy to sustain balance of payments surpluses throughout this period. After registering trade surplus increases most years from 1993 to 1998, a sharp drop followed from 1998 to 1999, in contrast to the others, who registered sharp increases. China was, of course, the only country in this list that did not devalue its currency in response to the financial crisis of 1997.

Source: IMF *Direction of Trade Statistics Yearbook* (Washington D.C., 2001)

Becoming the consumer of last resort has no doubt greatly reinforced America's hegemonic position in Asia. But continuing this role makes a quick and substantial reduction of America's external deficit dangerous.[20] If the emerging euro does make financing that deficit increasingly costly, America's Asian economic hegemony will grow increasingly dependent on financial cooperation from the EU.

HEGEMONY IN DECLINE?

America's economic hegemony has always been closely related to its broader geopolitical hegemony. While the collapse of the Soviet Union may have left the US as the only remaining military superpower, general historical trends suggest a more plural system in the offing. The European Union, liberated from the Soviet threat, hopes to expand its membership eastward and has been streamlining its governing structures and enlarging its common action to include collective diplomacy and defence. Russia, despite its disarray in the 1990s, is freed from its hopelessly dysfunctional Soviet system and Cold War isolation. It probably has much better long-term prospects – both for developing its still huge resources and for manoeuvring diplomatically. In Asia, the accumulating progress of China also suggests a relative shift in the global balance of forces. India is in the wings. Meanwhile, Japan – the original Asian great power of modern times – has grown more and more uncomfortable in the present global dispensation.

America's power has been eroding not only from external competition but also from internal disintegration. Successful hegemony depends not only on comparative power and wealth but also on national values, will, and competence. To succeed at global leadership requires, among other things, a political system that pays attention to the rest of the world. It requires sensitivity to the interests and sentiments of others, as well as a willingness, on critical occasions, to sacrifice national interests for the benefit of the system as a whole. The United States has met these requirements throughout much of the Cold War era. Hence the deep reservoir of legitimacy upon which the United States has been able to draw in moments of international crisis. But installing this internationalist bias in American Cold-War policy did require a major shift in America's political culture and constitutional system. The postwar international role of the US meant the primacy of American internationalism over American isolationism. And it meant the ascendancy of the American Presidency over other branches of the government.

With the Johnson and Nixon administrations of the 1960s, however, the pendulum began swinging back. The Congress and the courts, together with the states, grew determined to cut the Presidency down to its pre-imperial size. Thus, while the Clinton administration had its own particular problems, the Congressional and legal assault against it was part of a familiar and long-standing pattern that had persisted over at least seven administrations. It should not, therefore, be considered a passing whim of the political system. The circumstances of George W. Bush's election did not seem to promise a strong revival for the imperial Presidency.

Waning presidential authority was accompanied by the steady disintegration of the great imperial institutions of the Cold War – the State Department, the Pentagon and the CIA. All have tended to be taken over by their bureaucratic oligarchs and colonized by Congress – often at the behest of private interests or various ethnic lobbies – a process not without parallels to what occurred in Russia after the Soviet demise. Along with the decline of the Presidency and its instruments came a rebirth of isolationism, recast as unilateralism. Its overriding concern has been to reduce America's dependency on anyone else – to protect the nation's capacity to act as the national interest requires, without the need for allies or fear of effective reprisal from enemies. As a result, American policy has tended to become the assertion of hegemonic power without the discipline of genuinely hegemonic leadership. Following the atrocities of September 2001, the US has sought to use the 'war on terrorism' to 'relegitimize' its international hegemony – at home and abroad. Whatever the short-term successes, they seem unlikely to reverse the pluralist trends of the post-Cold War world. With luck, America's coalition building will prompt a revival of genuinely multilateral diplomacy. Otherwise, the US risks setting itself against the likely history of this century. The US becomes a 'hegemon in decline'.[21]

MULTILATERALISM THE CURE?

In a highly integrated world growing more plural, and showing persistent tendencies toward chaos, having an embattled and distracted hegemon suggests a dangerous future. Probably the most efficacious recourse is to enmesh the hegemon and the other major powers in multilateral international agreements and organizations. These can enlist other powers in the hegemon's labour and, at the same time, strengthen national governments, including the hegemon's, against disruptive internal interests. Europe's nation states, for example, have used the European Union not only to unite themselves for external action but also to discipline their own national parliaments from overspending and their central banks from inflating. Indeed, this is the good side of the EU's 'democratic deficit'.

In the US, the Presidency tries to use international agreements to protect its diplomacy from the depredations of rapacious Congressional cabals, greedy state governments, or parochial courts. By comparison with the EU states, however, the US has had less success with this tactic. American behaviour in recent years toward the UN, the IMF, the World Bank or the World Court hardly suggests a deep appreciation for their usefulness. Congress, no doubt, senses the threat that international organizations pose to its own independence, and to the buccaneering special interests that it often represents. Nevertheless, recurring global financial crises and military demands should logically encourage a new American appreciation for the benefits of multilateral institutions. Throughout the 1990s, for example, the International Monetary Fund (IMF) provided both a political cover and a technocratic instrument for trying to impose Western policies on Russia and other 'transforming' economies. In the late 1990s, the IMF also proved highly useful for organizing rescues of foundering currencies and banking systems around the world. In most instances, the US had the principal role in shaping the actual policies. Nevertheless, American unilateralism was constrained: initiatives had to be framed within the context of IMF rules; negotiations were needed to gain support from principal allies. The international bureaucracy proved reasonably adept at carrying out the policies once they had been agreed. 'Conditionality', exercised by a technocratic international civil service, was doubtless less obnoxious than tutelage imposed directly by the US. Criticism of the IMF was frequently criticism deflected away from the US itself.

In recent years, a great deal of hope has been invested in the new World Trade Organization (WTO), a rejuvenated GATT to manage today's exploding volumes of world trade. Trade disputes between the US, Europe and Japan have grown uncomfortably confrontational. The WTO, with its quasi-judicial adjudicating panels, guided by a corpus of agreed rules and principles, is supposed to inhibit flagrant assertions of special national interests and encourage more rational and consistent trade settlements. Among the affluent states, the prospects are probably not too bad. But the WTO also aspires to create rules and procedures acceptable to poor countries, above all to the newly powerful poor states, China in particular. China must be accommodated, it is said, lest the world repeat the self-destructive mistakes of the early twentieth century, when Britain and France failed to make room for a rising Germany. Bringing China into the WTO thus seems an ambitious leap toward global inclusiveness and appeasement. The aim is laudable, but is it reasonable?

MULTILATERAL CONSENSUS OR GLOBAL CLEAVAGE?

In the end, the success of multilateral institutions depends on a working consensus among at least the most powerful members, preferably a consensus that makes the authority of the institution seem legitimate to most participants. Such a consensus depends on generating a sufficient concordance of distinct interests and dispersed power. While achieving such harmony is difficult enough among the rich and Westernized advanced countries, it seems still more visionary within the emerging global system as a whole.[22] For all its dynamism, that global system has developed a profoundly skewed distribution of wealth and population. According to the World Bank's calculations, countries with a high, 'Western' standard of living – those with per capita incomes averaging over $20000 – make up only 15 per cent of the world's population. 'Middle income' states – those with per capita incomes averaging at least $2 990 – form another quarter. The remaining 60 per cent are 'low-income' countries.[23]

Looking inside the World Bank's abstraction – 'low income' countries – reveals a fact of major geopolitical significance. China and India together form roughly two-thirds of the population of the entire category. Thus, when we speak of the world's poorest 60 per cent, it is useful to remember that, within a few decades, two-thirds of them may be citizens of a superpower. If adjusted for purchasing power, China is already said to have the world's second largest economy.[24] The carefully framed projections of Angus Maddison see its adjusted GDP slightly exceeding that of the US by 2015. But even if China may soon have the aggregate income of a superpower, with substantially greater military and technological resources than at present, its citizens will still be very poor in world terms. Maddison's projections for 2015 foresee a Chinese adjusted GDP per capita of $6398, as opposed to $30 268 for the US, $25 533 for Japan, $22 199 for '32 Advanced Capitalist' countries, and $3 120 for India.[25] Thus, even after China's GDP exceeds that of the US, America's income per capita will remain five times greater than China's and ten times greater than India's.

Such radical differences are hardly new between the world's rich and poor countries. Formerly, however, the grievances of even the biggest poor countries could be ignored because they were also weak. Having countries like China or India among the ranks of the world's economic and military giants threatens to empower very large numbers of the world's poor. There is an obvious anomaly between being a nascent superpower and having a population with so disproportionately small a share of the world's comforts. A powerful demand for a more equal distribution of the world's wealth seems only natural. But how could a significantly more equal distribution be brought about without tearing the global political economy to pieces?

REDISTRIBUTION: ACCOMMODATING CHINA

Given the huge size of the poor populations, and the radically different ratios of population and wealth between rich and poor countries, a 'zero sum' redistribution bringing poor but powerful countries like China or India to anything like Western levels of per capita income implies a severe decline in the living standards of many others. Obviously, it seems better to achieve redistribution favouring the poor primarily through rapid growth, ideally so that everyone is better off, even if the poor gain disproportionately more. Rapid growth of this sort has gone on in many parts of the world throughout the postwar era. Several countries in Asia have been able to pass from poverty to relative affluence in a few decades. Some, like Japan, Hong Kong or Singapore, have reached or surpassed Western levels of per capita income. While Western labour has faced very considerable competition and displacement from this process, the overall consequences have been benign. Wages have risen sharply and new markets have been created in the Asian countries; compensating new industries and services have sprung up in the West and production has grown more efficient worldwide. Benefits to the West itself can be said to have greatly outweighed the costs.

China, however, exists in a different order of magnitude from Asia's 'little tigers'. With over 1.2 billion citizens, it is radically more populous. Even Japan has only 126 million inhabitants, a smaller population than France and Germany combined – 141 million. Thanks to China's radically larger population, raising China's per capita income requires very high aggregate growth. China has, of course, been growing rapidly since the beginning of its reform in 1978. From 1978 to 1995, its per capita income rose by 6 per cent a year. Maddison's projection, where China surpasses the US GDP in 2015, assumes an average per capita growth rate of only 4.5 per cent.[26] In short, so far at least, Maddison's projected rate of per capita growth seems conservative. Still, his projection shows China not only tripling its own GDP from 1995 to 2015 but thereby also adding to the world economy an amount roughly equal to the entire US GDP of 1995. Even so, Maddison reckons, China's GDP per capita, adjusted for purchasing power, will still be only one fifth that of the US. In other words, to reach the same level of per capita income as the US in 2015, China would need a GDP five times as large as America's.

China's low per capita income is not only very low by Western standards, but is poor by East Asian standards as well. While, except for Japan, Taiwan, tiny Hong Kong and Singapore, the Asian tigers themselves remain poor by Western standards of per capita income, they are rich compared to China. Their wage levels are much higher, and, incidentally, not necessarily offset by higher productivity per worker.

Figures like those in Table 3.3, showing Chinese competitiveness to be high and per capita income very low, suggest that Chinese growth has a long way to run.

Why then should rapid Chinese growth stop, even when the GDP reaches the size of the American? There are, of course, many possible answers. Calculations that extrapolate from past performance are obviously conjectural. They do, however, show the enormous growth required to raise China's per capita income even to the level of the Asian tigers. Rapid growth of such magnitude is unlikely to occur without very considerable domestic economic, social and political disruption. China has a very large but generally inefficient and loss-making sector of state-owned businesses, employing a large part of the urban population.[27] This sector is massively subsidized by the banking system, whose asset base is therefore problematic. The fiscal position of the central government itself is weak – thanks to undeveloped tax collection and a welter of tax concessions. In 1995, for example, government revenue was only 11 per cent of GDP and government debt was growing rapidly. Nevertheless, since 1978 the Chinese government has generally shown great skill in juggling the contradictions of its mixed economic system and in managing the social and political disruptions of rapid transition. But the task will not necessarily grow easier as the disruptions accumulate. Meanwhile Tiananmen Square stands as an indicator of how violent the consequences of breakdown might be.

Assuming China's internal problems can somehow be managed, China's huge growth will have numerous unsettling consequences for the rest of the world economy. Continuing China's growth at anything like Maddison's pace would presumably absorb a larger and larger share of the world's capital and raw materials.[28] It can be argued, of course, that China – with its high savings rate – would itself generate a great deal of the new capital required. China's energy needs, however, seem a more intractable challenge.[29] China is already the world's second largest consumer of energy, after the US. Between 1978 and 1993, China's total final energy consumption more than doubled. It is expected to have doubled again by 2006.[30]

China is a fast-growing consumer of oil. From 1990 to 1998, its oil use roughly doubled; since 1993, it has been a net importer. China is, moreover, the world's largest producer and consumer of coal, which accounts for 35 per cent of the country's primary energy consumption.[31] Although coal's relative significance is expected to diminish, demand for it is still projected to double by the year 2020. The ecological consequences are not pleasant to contemplate.

Table 3.3: Comparative National Statistics

	Population, 1999 (thousands)	GDP per capita, 1999 (US $)	PPP GDP per capita, 1999 (purchasing power parity in US $)	Labor cost per worker in manufacturing 1990-1994 (US $)	Value added per worker, 1990-1994 (U.S.$)	Ratio of value-added to labor cost, 1990-1994
China	1 253 595	789	3 617	729	2 885	3.95
U.S.	278 230	32 894	31 871	28 907	81 353	2.81
Japan	126 570	34 344	24 898	31 687	92 815	2.92
Thailand	60 246	2 064	6 132	2 705	19 946	7.37
South Korea	46 858	8 684	15 712	10 743	40 916	3.38
Malaysia	22 710	3 371	8 208	3 429	12 661	3.69
Singapore	3 952	21494	20 766	21 543	40 674	1.88

Note: Using 1995 figures adjusted for purchasing power, Maddison calculates that China's per capita income was 13 per cent of that in Japan, 20 per cent of that in Taiwan, 22 per cent of that in Korea and 11 per cent of that in the US. Maddison, op. cit., p. 17.

Source: The World Bank Group, http://www.worldbank.org/data/databytopic/keyrefs.html, http://www.worldbank.org/data/wdi2001/pdfs/tab2_5.pdf

Table 3.4: China, US and EU Energy Consumption and CO_2 Pollution

	Total Final Energy Consumption (KTOE)			Energy Consumption Per Capita (TOE)			CO_2 Per Capita (t)		Total CO_2 (Mt)
	1971	1990	1998	1990	1998	1971	1998	1998
CHINA	185 412	484 032	745 954	0.43	0.60	1.02	2.30	2 852
US	1 235 685	1 306 271	1 431 549	5.23	5.31	20.70	20.10	5 409
EU	772 382	929 993	1 027 957	2.55	2.75	8.95	8.47	3 170

Source: International Energy Agency Data Services, 2001, www.iea.org.

Notes: *KTOE: Thousand tons of oil equivalent; TOE: Tons of oil equivalent; t: ton; Mt: Megaton.*

Table 3.5: China, US and EU Oil Consumption and Importation

	Total Petroleum Product Use (KTOE)			Total Consumption per Million (KTOE)			Crude Oil Imports (1000 t)		
	1971	1990	1998	1971	1990	1998	1971	1990	1998
CHINA	27 887	82 572	162 845	33.16	72.75	131.47		2 923	27 320
U.S.	640 363	697 838	777 060	3 078.67	2 791.35	2 888.69		314 165	464 416
EU	477 612	474 399	531 445	1 396.52	1 303.29	1 420.97		458 670	555 502

Source: International Energy Agency Data Services, 2001, www.iea.org

Notes: KTOE: Thousand tons of oil equivalent; t: ton.

China, of course, is not the only populous state on its way to military and political empowerment. India is another nascent superpower, even poorer, and with a population soon expected to exceed China's. What will happen if India begins growing as rapidly as China?[32] It may certainly be argued that Chinese and Indians have as much right to pollute the world, or bid up the price of oil, as the Americans or Europeans. But for those, East and West, who suffer the consequences of introducing another billion or two people to Western energy practices, such arguments may offer little consolation.

In summary, expecting gradual and benevolent growth to ameliorate substantially the world's present radical inequality of incomes requires robust faith in the future. Unassisted by faith, reason also suggests grimmer possibilities: dramatic domestic social and political instability, growth that radically alters the planet's ecosystem, radical impoverishment of the West or international conflicts reminiscent of the early twentieth century. Under such circumstances, sustaining a global consensus for rules-based multilateral organizations to manage the world's economy seems a difficult project. A shifting political, military, and economic balance gradually empowering the world's poor states suggests difficult times ahead for global governance.

PRACTICAL CONCLUSIONS

The great self-destructive quarrels of the earlier twentieth century were principally among the rich Western nations themselves. Even the postwar world economy – for all its rapidly spreading prosperity – has had structural problems threatening to get out of control. For a long time, a generally benevolent American hegemon has managed the various crises, one way or another. The end of the bipolar Cold War marks the advent of a more balanced and complex world system. Like the European states in 1910, today's West is no longer alone in the world of power. It will not be enough for the West simply to end its old internecine quarrels. Given the mutually destructive character of a planetary war, the West must also come to terms with the world's newly empowered poor as generously as it can. None of this will be easy.

With huge China galloping forward into the global economy, the Malthusian catastrophes implicit in rapid 'modernization' seem increasingly real and immediate. The world's future doubtless does depend on whether the West can successfully accommodate Asia's huge and hungry great powers into the global system. But the strategy so often preferred for China – fast integration accompanied by rapid democratization – seems dubious. Something more subtle and complex is required than a simple-minded extension of Western consumerist values to the world at large.

Given the broad fears among environmentalists that even the present level of world development is far from sustainable, the West's consumerist paradigm, with its colossal waste, is not necessarily a good long-term strategy for China's future. Perhaps China can develop a better model for the planet. We can only hope that we in the West, as well as the Chinese, have the cultural depth and moral imagination to meet the dangerous period of radical adjustment that lies ahead. The predictable pressures of rapid Asian development suggest that Americans and Europeans must begin to take a serious long-term view of how to reform their own economies. To survive, Western democracy may have to base itself on values other than those that imply ever-greater abundance. Given the intractable problems that lie ahead, today's facile consumerism may soon grow painfully inappropriate. Susan's Casino may be closing down.

Considering the world from this perspective suggests the fatuousness of 'peace theory' or other triumphalist Western visions that see history progressing effortlessly to more and more global integration, complete with democracy and mushrooming prosperity for all. More likely, the West will be challenged to cut back its own consumerism – not only by Nature but also by the rest of mankind.

There is, of course, always the Micawber Option: something may turn up. For two centuries, science and technology have been rescuing the world from its long-predicted Malthusian fate. Today, we can easily dream of some new form of energy to allow us to sidestep the grim global struggle over redistribution that now seems so difficult to avoid. History, we can reassure ourselves, seldom chooses apocalyptic alternatives. It, nevertheless, seems prudent to take a more sober view of the future. We should not forget the terrible lacerations that the world inflicted on itself by failing to make timely adjustments in the century just past. If we do not anticipate and master our own looming problems, there seems no good reason to presume that the horrors of our new century will be any less than those of the last.

NOTES

1. See Charles P. Kindleberger, *The World in Depression 1929–1939* (Berkeley: University of California Press, 1973) and 'Systems of International Organization' in David P. Calleo (ed.), *Money and the Coming World Order* (New York: New York University Press, 1976). See also Robert Gilpin, *War and Change in International Politics* (New York: Cambridge University Press, 1981). Over the past two decades, theories of hegemonic stability have grown increasingly sophisticated. Scholars emphasize the significance of networks and structures of cooperation which provide the institutional framework for hegemons to lead and all countries to act in a collectively optimal manner (see for example Robert O. Keohane, *After Hegemony: Cooperation and Discord in the World Political Economy* (Princeton, NJ: Princeton University Press, 1984). Kindleberger himself has acknowledged the significance of what might be called post-hegemonic stability theories' (see his 'International Public

Goods without International Government,' *American Economic Review*, vol. 76, no. 1 (1986), pp.1–13).

2. In 1992 dollars, US military spending fell from $298 billion in 1992 to $239 billion in 1997, a drop of 20 per cent. Calculated from 1987, the ten-year decline was 28 per cent in real terms, *Budget of the United States Government: Historical Tables*, Fiscal Year 1999, (Washington DC: US Government Printing Office, 1998) pp.108–09.

3. *Economic Report of the President, 2001*, (Washington DC: US Government Printing Office, 2001) p. 163, *OECD Historical Statistics 2000, 1970–1999*, (Paris: OECD, 2001) p. 51. For a good summary of the issues see IMF, *World Economic Outlook, October 2000* (Washington, DC: International Monetary Fund, 2000), pp. 48ff. There are, of course, sceptical views about increasing productivity based on computerization. See Robert J. Gordon, 'Does the "New Economy" Measure Up to the Great Inventions of the Past?,' *NBER Working Paper*, no. 7833, (Cambridge, MA: National Bureau of Economic Research, 2000). See also Alan Cane, 'Interview Paul Strassmann: Guru who sees no profit in computers,' *Financial Times*, 28 June 2001, p. 9.

4. The US current account deficit was $77 billion in 1990 and is estimated at $470.5 billion in 2001. The trade deficit was $109 billion in 1990 and is estimated to be $490.5 billion for 2001, *OECD Economic Outlook, December 2000* (Paris: OECD, 2000), pp. 259, 256. For the Clinton Administration's views of the causes and consequences of the external deficit, see *Economic Report of the President, 2001*, Chapter 4, especially pp. 158ff.

5. For a fuller discussion, see D.P. Calleo, *The Bankrupting of America*, (New York: William Morrow and Co., 1992), Chapter 6.

6. The US may instead increase its money supply more rapidly and thereby force down the dollar's exchange rate. How much this improved the trade deficit would presumably depend, *inter alia*, on whether it also resulted in increased demand and price inflation in the domestic economy. In any event, a falling dollar with low real interest rates would probably not encourage investors or savers to remain in dollars. For various views about the consequences of the euro, see Martin Feldstein, 'EMU and International Conflict', *Foreign Affairs*, vol. 76, no. 6, November/December 1997 and 'The Political Economy of the European Economic and Monetary Union: Political Sources of an Economic Liability', *Journal of Economic Perspectives*, Fall 1997; C. Fred Bergsten, 'The Coming Euro-Dollar Clash,' *Foreign Affairs*, vol. 78, no. 2, March/April 1999: and my 'The Strategic Implications of the Euro,' *Survival*, Spring 1999, vol. 41, no. 1, pp. 5–19.

7. For ESDI, see Philip Gordon, *US and ESDI in the New NATO* (Paris: Institut français des relations internationales, 1998). For a lengthy analysis of Europe's efforts at defence cooperation, see my *Rethinking Europe's Future* (Princeton, NJ: Princeton University Press, 2001), Chapter 14.

8. For the complex and interrelated causes of America's growing budget and current account deficits, see Stephen Marris, *Deficits and Dollars: The World Economy at Risk*, updated edition, Analyses in International Economics No. 14 (Washington DC, Institute for International Economics, 1987) pp. xiv–xlvii, 3–13, 42–50. For my own attempt to analyse US fiscal deficits during the Cold War, see *The Bankrupting of America*, op. cit., Chs 2–5.

9. Despite the large current account deficit, a balanced fiscal budget seemed to produce the effects that its votaries had always promised. With the government no longer soaking up domestic capital for its own deficits, capital was available for private borrowers and rapid growth ensued. For my own analysis of Clinton's fiscal policy and the American boom of the 1990's, see *Rethinking Europe's Future*, op. cit., Ch. 11.

10. Nor will they be forced to, so long as Europeans continue to pour their investment capital into the US. It remains to be seen whether a recession and falling stock market could bring the foreign inflow of capital to an end, as the nascent euro becomes a reality. Moreover, the Bush administration's tax cuts of 2001 may end government saving; *ceteris paribus*, absorption should tend to rise and the external deficit to deteriorate further, etc. For seeming evidence of capital flows see UNCTAD, 'FDI Downturn in 2001 Touches Almost All Regions,' TAD/INF/PR 36, 21 January 2002 (http://www.unctad.org/en/press/pdfs/pr01_36.en.pdf) and UNCTAD, *World Investment Report 2001*, (Geneva: UNCTAD, 2001), Chapter 1.

11. Deficits are also significant and growing rapidly with Canada, Mexico, and even with Europe.
12. See Robert Rubin, 'Hearing of Senate Foreign Relations Committee on IMF and Asian Financial Crisis', *Federal News Service*, 12 February, 1998.
13. Explanations of recent currency crises usually stress the role of either macroeconomic fundamentals or of speculative attacks and 'contagion'. The Russian, Asian and Brazilian crises appear to have reflected a combination of the two: poor fundamentals – including excessive exchange rate appreciation – plus adverse market sentiment. In the Asia crises, Paul Krugman notes the moral hazard arising from implicit government guarantees for bank liabilities, which induced banks to lend excessively to firms, and thus induced an asset price bubble which subsequently burst. For an overview of recent currency crises, see *IMF World Economic Outlook, May 1999* (Washington, DC: International Monetary Fund, 1999), esp. pp. 66–87.   For Paul Krugman's views, see, his 'What Happened to Asia?' http://web.mit.edu/krugman/www. DISINTER.html. For other analyses of the Asian crisis, see, *inter alia*, Morris Goldstein, *The Asian Financial Crisis: Causes, Cures and Systemic Implications*, Policy Analyses in International Economics 55 (Washington, DC: Institute for International Economics, 1998); Stephen Radelet and Jeffrey Sachs, *The East Asian Financial Crisis: Diagnosis, Remedies, Prospects*, Brookings Papers on Economic Activity, (Washington, DC: Brookings Institution, 1998); Martin Feldstein, 'A Self-Help Guide for Emerging Markets,' *Foreign Affairs*, March 1999. For a view that I find particularly convincing and suggestive, see Benedict Anderson, 'From Miracle to Crash,' *London Review of Books*, vol. 20, no. 8, 1998. For Susan Strange's discussion of the causes of the financial crisis in Asia and its contagion throughout the region, see *Mad Money* (Manchester: Manchester University Press, 1998), pp. 108–112.
14. John Williamson and Molly Mahar, 'A Survey of Financial Liberalization', *Essays in International Finance* 211, November 1998 and Joseph Stiglitz, 'Capital Market Liberalization, Economic Growth, and Instability', *World Development* 28, pp.1075–1086, 2000.
15. *Economic Report of the President, 2001*, op. cit., p. 400. IMF, *World Economic Outlook, October 2000*, op. cit., p 202.
16. World Bank, *2000 World Development Indicators CD-ROM*.
17. Maddison, op.cit., p. 88. Comparable figures for Japan are 19.3 per cent of exports going to the US in 1978 and 20.4 per cent in 1996; for Western Europe 12.5 per cent and 13.7 per cent. Figures are complicated by re-exports from Hong Kong. See Nicholas R. Lardy, *China in the World Economy*, (Washington, DC: Institute for International Economics, 1994), p. 76.
18. Benedict Anderson, 'From Miracle to Crash', *London Review of Books*, vol. 20, no. 8, 1998. Maddison argues, however, that the world economy should be able to absorb China's exports and notes that in 1996, they were only 3 per cent of the world's total, 11 per cent of Asia's, less than those of either Belgium or the Netherlands, and furthermore, China's rapid growth would produce a corresponding increase in imports. It may be noted, however, that whereas the euro area countries increased their real GDP from 1992 to 1999 by roughly 1.6 per cent per annum, China's increased by roughly 10.5 per cent per annum. IMF, *World Economic Outlook, October 2000*, op. cit., pp. 200, 205. Maddison, op. cit., p 17. For a recent discussion, see Michael Richardson, 'China's Growth Weighs on Neighboring Countries', *International Herald Tribune*, 18–19 August, 2001, p. 1.
19. World dollar prices of manufactures fell by a cumulative 12 per cent between 1996 and 1998; non-oil commodities fell by 19 per cent, and oil by 41 per cent, *IMF World Economic Outlook, May 1999* (Washington DC, International Monetary Fund, 1998), p. 167.
20. For a recent discussion of the vulnerability of Asian economies to a drop in US trade, see Richard McGregor and Peronet Despeignes, 'U.S. slowdown buffets Taiwan: Asian Bellwether reports worst GDP fall in 25 years as downturn continues to bite worldwide,' *Financial Times*, 18/19 August 2001, p. 1.
21. For a discussion of the concept of a 'hegemon in decline', see David P. Calleo, *Beyond American Hegemony*, (New York: Basic Books, 1987) pp. 131ff. See also Barry Buzan, *Peoples, States, and Fear: The National Security Problem in International Relations* (Chapel Hill: University of North Carolina Press, 1983), 136–50.

22. For an attempt to explain the significance of the growing difficulties among advanced Western countries, particularly in trade concerning 'high technology,' see my *Rethinking Europe's Future*, op. cit., Chapter 12.

23. World Bank, *2000 World Development Indicators CD-ROM*. Furthermore, the World Bank estimates that of the world's 6 billion people, 2.8 billion live on less than $2 a day. 1.2 billion live on less than $1 a day, with 44 per cent of the poorest living in South Asia. The average income in the richest 20 countries is 37 times the average in the poorest 20 – and that gap has doubled over the last 40 years (see World Bank, *World Development Report 2000/2001* (Oxford: Oxford University Press, 2000), pp. 3–4. See also Jeffrey D. Sachs, Andrew D. Mellinger and John L. Gallup, 'The Geography of Poverty and Wealth', *Scientific American* vol. 284, no. 3, pp. 71–75, 2001.

24. Using purchasing power parity (PPP) figures. Otherwise, based on current exchange rates, it is seventh – after the US, Japan, Germany, United Kingdom, France and Italy (1999 figures). See World Bank website, http://www.worldbank.org/data/databytopic/keyrefs.html.

25. Angus Maddison, *Chinese Economic Performance in the Long-Run*, (Paris: OECD, 1998) p. 97.

26. Taking IMF real growth figures, adjusted for population growth, shows China's real GDP growth per capita since 1995 as follows: 9.6 per cent (1996), 8.8 per cent (1997), 7.8 per cent (1998), 7.1 per cent (1999). IMF estimates 7.5 per cent (2000) and 7.3 per cent (2001). For the unadjusted real GDP growth figures, see IMF, *World Economic Outlook*, October 2000, op. cit., pp. 22. For current population figures, see World Bank website, http://www.worldbank.org/data/databytopic/keyrefs.html.

27. Some 67 million workers were said to be employed in state-owned enterprises in 1996. Output per worker in these industries was less than three-quarters of the national average. For a further discussion of China's obstacles to rapid growth, see Maddison, op. cit., pp. 17–18, 81, 90–96.

28. For further discussions, see World Bank, *1998 World Development Indicators*, p. 171.

29. See also 'China Country Analysis Brief', Energy Information Administration, April 2001. http://www.eia.doe.gov/emeu/cabs/china.html, Ibid. From 1980 to 1997, China's commercial energy use jumped from the equivalent of 609 million metric tons of oil to 1.1 billion metric tons – an average annual increase of 4 per cent. US use in 1997 stood at 2.2 billion tons – an increase of 1.4 per cent since 1980. See Verne W. Louse and Ian McCreary, 'China's Energy – A Forecast to 2015', *Los Alamos National Laboratory International Economics Report* LA-UR–96–2972, September 1996.

30. 'Many experts feel that China's water problem poses an ever bigger challenge, risking (among other things) China's ability to keep scaling up its food production to feed its still increasing population. See for example Carmen Revenga, Jake Brunner, Norbert Henninger, Ken Kassem, Richard Payne, *Pilot Analysis of Global Ecosystems: Freshwater Systems* (Washington, DC: World Resources Institute 2001) and also World Resources Institute, *Earthtrends Data Source*, 2001, available at http://www.wri.org/.

31. See International Energy Agency, *Energy Balances Non-OECD Countries, 2000 Edition*.

32. For a recent view on why India's growth is slower than China's, see Edward Luce, 'Indian growth still frustratingly poor as plans for reform fail to get underway', *Financial Times*, 17 August 2001, p. 5. But for India's potential strength, see Augus Donald, Khozem Merchant and Tom Foremski, 'Growth in Indian software exports,' Ibid.

4. Global Poverty and the Rich-Country Racket

Jochen Lorentzen

Between 1.2 and 2.8 billion people in the world are very poor, depending on how one counts. Most of them live in a developing country. Take your pick: this is bad luck; the result of wrong policies (perhaps administered by incompetent or corrupt elites); a merely temporary cost of market liberalisation; or, finally, the consequence of a rich-country racket that withholds the benefits of open markets from those who need them most. A child born into an area highly susceptible to debilitating diseases and likely to die before it ever gets a chance to reflect what it wants to do when it grows up, has the cards stacked against it: bad luck. A mother who reacts to rising primary school fees by sending her kids to work instead, forgoes both her own retirement security and the children's chance to learn what it takes to escape from poverty: wrong (social and education) policy. A smallholder who accepts a better-paying job on a large but distant farm and spends an exorbitant amount of time on the commute because the private sector response to a demonopolized transport sector takes time to develop, has good reasons to believe that things will get better: temporary disadvantage. A garment manufacturer or sugar cane grower faced with export barriers in the rich countries plays his part in minimizing the adjustment in those places that most tout, and benefit from, world-wide market opening: rich-country racket. Unfortunately not much can be done about bad luck. Fundamentally not much *needs* to be done, although they always can be cushioned, about temporary costs of adapting to a changing world. By contrast, wrong policies can, and should be, corrected. What about the racket?

This chapter discusses the inconsistency with which rich countries promote globalization, and how they attempt to appropriate the resulting gains while pushing the necessary costs onto poor countries, breaking their own rules along the way. It argues that the rich countries have managed to have their cake and eat it, exacerbating poverty in the world. Susan Strange claimed that the diffusion of authority away from national governments left some things simply ungoverned that had been regulated in the past and should be so in the present (1996, 14). But what rich-country governments do does indeed influence poverty, and so the case at hand is not one of '*un'*- but of *mis*governance. Governance, according to the Oxford English Dictionary, is the 'action or manner of governing', 'regulating influence', 'good order', 'system of regulations' (1989). Thus, tomorrow's weather is not a question of governance. By contrast, climate change is. Misgovernance is the opposite: the absence, or the wrongful administration, of rules aimed at facilitating the achievement of some clearly stated goals in an orderly fashion. Therefore, that some people are born into a harsh life somewhere in South Asia while others are born into a privileged existence somewhere in Europe, has nothing to do with misgovernance. But if rich-country governments, contrary to the letter – let alone the spirit – of international agreements, make it harder for the former to do something about their fate, we have a case of misgoverned poverty.

THE POOR IN THE WORLD

In 1998, 56 per cent of world households consumed less than $2.15 per person per day. By this simple definition of dollar poverty, poverty rose during the 1990s. This is in marked contrast to 1970–90 when poverty – and hunger, premature death, and illiteracy that go with it – actually retreated substantially. Most of the poor live in South and East Asia (71 per cent), followed by Sub-Saharan Africa (17 per cent), Latin America and the Caribbean (6 per cent), Eastern Europe and Central Asia (3 per cent), and the Middle East and North Africa (2 per cent). The number of poor declined by 14 per cent in East Asia in 1990–98; in all other regions it increased, especially in Africa (22 per cent) and Eastern Europe and Central Asia where it more than doubled (Chen and Ravallion 2000).

Three-quarters of the poor live in rural areas and depend on agriculture for making a living. This share will decline but is expected to be still at 50 per cent in 2025 (IFAD 2001). The lives of the rural poor revolve around staple goods. What they produce, they sell cheaply during the glut after harvest because of their dire need for cash. Then they buy at high prices during the lean season which makes them doubly vulnerable. They spend up to four-fifths of their income on staples which often does not suffice for sound health or for getting efficiently through the day – some 800 million people are undernourished. What is left does not cover the needs for adequate clothing, housing, schooling, or health care. Thus, approximately one billion people in developing countries live in unacceptable housing or completely lack adequate shelter, 1.4 billion do not have access to safe water, and 2.9 billion go without access to adequate sanitation, all of which makes good hygiene as good as impossible. This means life is tough today and no better tomorrow because the underinvestment in anything but subsistence restricts earning potential and impairs people's health. Poverty, according to the World Health Organization, is thus the world's biggest killer (WHO 2000).

Extreme poverty afflicts four out of ten children born in the developing world. One hundred and seventy million do not get enough to eat, and many suffer lack of clean water and inadequate sanitation. As a consequence, they will not live to become very old. Eleven million children die each year from diseases that for the most part are preventable. But before she dies, a girl born poor is likely to become an adolescent mother of another underweight baby, with yet another future of deprivation ahead of it (UNICEF 2001).

There is a lot of disagreement about the causes of poverty. But at the same time, there is also a consensus that the presence of abject poverty is wrong, and that something should be done about it. The 2000 UN Millennium Summit pledged the halving of extreme poverty, namely the numbers of those living on less than $1 a day at purchasing power parity, in 1995–2015. UN targets from 1995 also included the enrolment of all children in primary school and the reduction of infant mortality rates by two-thirds. From 1996 international donors and financial institutions, including the World Bank and the IMF, agreed to make poverty reduction a priority in their programmes. Yet the world is not on track on these targets. For example, only some ten million people escape poverty every year. This is less than a third of the rate required to halve poverty by 2015. If average GDP per capita growth rates reached in the 1990s by the world's 43 poorest countries – those with a per capita GDP of below $900 – continue into the future, only one of them is likely to graduate out of this group before 2015 (IFAD 2001, UNCTAD 2000b).

So what is going wrong? Much, is the short answer. The following sections provide details for a more complex explanation.

THE SCOURGE OF WORLD INEQUALITY

For the first time, household income and expenditure data have become available for a large number of countries in the world. Hence, instead of operating with not particularly meaningful national averages of income per capita, new research allows one to gauge the extent of 'true' inequality (Milanovic 2002). Unfortunately, the improved toolkit brings mostly bad news. In the early 1990s world inequality topped the historically high levels of the late 1980s. This is despite the 5.7 per cent rise in real world per capita income in 1988–93. Hence growth does not make everybody better off. Indeed the poorest 75 per cent of the people in the world lost out in absolute terms in the half-decade to 1993. The worst losers are across all income groups in Eastern Europe and the CIS, among the bottom half in Africa, and the bottom decile in Latin America and the Caribbean. By contrast, the richest 20 per cent of the world population improved their position by 12 per cent, twice as much as the increase in mean world income.

In 1993, Asia was the most unequal region, followed by Latin America and the Caribbean, Africa, and Eastern Europe and the CIS. Inequality was lowest in the developed market economies. Over time, increases in inequality in 1988–93 were worst in the transition economies (+81 per cent), Africa (+12 per cent), and Asia (+10 per cent), while income distributions became slightly more equal in both Latin America and the Caribbean and the developed countries.

Inequality depends, first, on who you are. Some countries have a relatively equal distribution of income and wealth, others less so. This 'within-country' inequality is not so important in Asia provided one distinguishes between the urban and rural populations in China and India. In general, inequality is relatively low in the most populous areas, such as Egypt, Algeria, or Morocco. It accounts for roughly a fifth of overall inequality in Latin America and the Caribbean, Eastern Europe and the CIS, and the developed countries. In 1988–93 it went down in all regions except the transition economies.

Inequality also depends, second, on where you live. Canadians are richer than Vietnamese and this is a principal determinant of world inequality. In fact, 'between-country' inequality explains two-thirds of inequality in Africa and 87 per cent in Asia. In 1988–93, it rose in Africa, Asia, and Eastern Europe and the CIS, meaning that at least some countries in those regions did not converge upward with the rest of the world but only downward with themselves.

Finally, inequality depends on the degree of homogeneity of a population. It is high if all the king's sons are rich or if all the beggar's daughters are poor. A Vietnamese truck driver who happens to be richer than his Canadian counterpart is relatively independent of who he is and where he lives – his income depends on factors other than class or place. Latin America and the Caribbean as well as the developed countries are the most homogeneous regions, Asia the least. The former two are also the only two regions where class and place matter less over time, where inequality is therefore on the retreat (Milanovic 2002).

Overall, within-country inequality has only a marginal influence on world inequality. This does not mean, for example, that income differentiation in the US is negligible. But on the world scale, countries with large total incomes, such as the US, have relatively small populations while those with small total incomes, such as China, have relatively large populations. Also, mean country incomes among poor countries are very close. Thus, it is between-country inequality that determines world inequality almost single-handedly, namely the difference between the G-7 countries at one end of the spectrum, and India and China at the other. And it is the slower growth in the rural areas of these populous, poor countries relative both to their urban centres and to select OECD economies that drove the increase in world inequality from the 1980s to the 1990s (Milanovic 2002).

Newer data indicate that inequality is not on the way out. Real annual per capita consumption in low- and middle-income countries grew by 2.6 per cent in the 1990s. Yet the number of poor rose. Why? Because empirically the chances of the very poor to leave poverty behind differ with respect to initial income inequalities. This means that high (and/or rising) inequality – along with your skills and where you live – is a constraint on growth. It also means that people in Africa, where depths of poverty are greatest, are in a bad starting position for changing their fate (Chen and Ravallion 2000). They certainly do not need a rich-country racket to make life even more difficult.

HOW TRADE LIBERALISATION MAY HURT THE POOR

Both the gains from trade and the differential impact on producers and consumers of these gains are well established. Reducing trade restrictions raises global welfare. Whether and to what extent people benefit from this depends on what they produce and what they consume, and on the time horizon, namely short- vs long-term effects. The public debate about the connection between trade and poverty is often simplistic and ideological. On the one hand, critics of more open markets maintain that the increased competition that comes with liberalized trade always hurts the poor. On the other, critics of policies restricting competition argue that the growth generated by liberalized trade always trickles down to the poor. Empirical evidence demonstrates that these simplistic views are wrong. A farmer who is freed from purchasing inputs at artificially high prices and allowed to export her produce instead of selling it at controlled prices to a government agency, can better exploit her productive potential. Over time this may allow her to invest in new facilities or acquire new equipment. Hence, demand spillovers positively affect local industries such as construction, simple manufactures, or domestic services all of which are employment intensive and provide jobs for the poor. The poor can thus enjoin the benefits of economic growth. But Control Risks Group, a security consultancy, warned in its *Outlook 2000* annual report that 'trade liberalisation is increasingly allowing multinationals to extract raw products and profits from developing countries, often at great environmental cost and with little benefit to anyone locally other than a wealthy oligarchy' (Cohen 1999). Hence, reality is complicated and not captured by general conclusions (Winters 2001). This section seeks to explain why, and how, trade liberalization may hurt the poor. It is not an argument against trade liberalization, but an attempt to show that reform policies, however well intentioned, may indeed exacerbate the plight of the poor.

Greater openness to trade may affect a significant chunk of the population negatively (Lundberg and Squire 1999). This is because those at the bottom of the income pyramid often are least equipped to adjust to greater openness. They have little education that would help them to understand and interpret structural change. They live in areas that are difficult to reach; consequently, contacts with outsiders, including traders, are cumbersome. For example, women with heavy family obligations who cannot just pack up and leave, suffer from high transport costs of perishable goods over poor roads to distant markets. And perhaps these people are not conversant in a majority language necessary to deal with market intermediaries, or they lack the clout to influence the terms of market participation. For example, unless farmers have proper access to credit to invest in the commercialization, marketing, or even diversification of their production, they rely on others for their sales, such as monopsonistic traders, who may then get an excess share of the profits. In addition, if rural inequality is pronounced and some or many rural folk are net food buyers, the higher prices for food that follow liberalization penalise them instead of winning them extra farm income. Finally, employment-intensive small farms may run into scale disadvantages compared to larger operations if the globalization of food chains introduces complicated requirements such as uniform product appearance or pesticide regulations (IFAD 2001).

Real-life stories of the poor bear out these general observations. In Zambia, rural poverty got worse after the government withdrew maize purchasing arrangements in the early 1990s. A third of the rural poor lived more than 20km from the nearest market and thus had a hard time getting its production to customers. Transport costs rose after the government stopped road maintenance and public transport became more infrequent. The immediate consequence was a drop of a third in smallholder income in 1991–94, with subsequent repercussions on school and health clinic attendance. The removal of price controls on agriculture resulted in a decline of maize production – clearly an unanticipated and undesired effect. Again, it was remote farmers who struggled to cope with the decline in subsidies. Also, the depreciation of the exchange rate – part of the reform package – affected the price of imported fertilizer more than that of maize. This deterioration in the terms of trade meant that farmers had to make do with less fertilizer which, in turn, translated into lower yields. For many, this led back into subsistence production. The way out into more valuable crops was not easy. Some maize growers shifted into cotton which is more labour-intensive than maize.

Women growers thus had less time for childcare and for growing household staples. Others failed to shift out of maize because a long tradition of cash-cropping had made them lose knowledge of how to produce alternative crops (Oxfam/IDS 1999).

Sub-Saharan countries have become important suppliers of horticultural commodities (vegetables, 'exotic' fruit, and cut flowers) to Europe. Kenya and Zimbabwe are the most successful exporters. This is not an easy trade. For products to end up on European supermarket shelves, they must comply with exacting quality criteria and regulatory requirements. The introduction of total quality management and just-in-time practices in horticultural commodity chains led to a rationalization of the supply base. In the early 1990s, smallholders in Kenya produced some three-quarters of the country's agricultural output which was eventually sold through wholesale markets. They have since been replaced by large-scale production units, and the top five exporters control about 75 per cent of fresh vegetable exports. To those producers and exporters that are part of the supply base, this offers lucrative possibilities through extending local control over quality, logistics, storage, distribution, transport, and a range of processing activities. Yet many small producers got marginalized because they cannot muster the asset-specific investments in equipment and systems (Dolan et al. 1999). In Central America, similarly, multinational corporations (MNCs) control the production of some 25 per cent of non-traditional export crops, along with much of distribution and transport. Smallholders do not grow these crops because their lack of access to credit, technology, and information prevents them from competing in this profitable trade (Thrupp 1995). If all or many of the smallholders had found work on large farms or in other sectors, there would not be a problem. And the statistics on poverty and inequality would not look so bleak.

In sum, the poor are more vulnerable to shifts in relative international prices in any event, and trade reform may exacerbate this vulnerability.

THE DOWNSIDE OF PARTICIPATING IN THE WORLD TRADE SYSTEM

The previous section illustrated how the gains of generally desirable economic reforms may bypass the poor and actually make life harder for them. This section shows how rich countries are more part of the problem than of the solution. It focuses on protectionism practised by advanced market economies, past and present.

In David Ricardo's world, countries and sectors have different factor endowments. This gives rise to divergent investment, production, and export patterns, leading to large mutual benefits from trade liberalization. In the real world of trade between OECD countries during the first three post-war decades, firms actually had increasingly similar factor endowments and, thus, converging cost structures. Therefore, the marginal price sensitivity of international trade rose, leading in principle to smaller gains from trade liberalization. The GATT reflected these realities in that it favoured intra-industry specialization. This was advantageous for the rich countries insofar as it accommodated domestic stabilization without incurring high adjustment costs. By contrast, inter-industry specialization did not really happen.

Why not? One explanation is that the majority of developing countries pursued import-substituting industrialization strategies. They were not interested in a true division of labour because they wanted to build up the very same industries as in the developed world. To this end they merely asked the GATT to excuse them from some of the disciplines they felt they could not, or did not want to, comply with. This is why they received what is called 'Differential and More Favourable Treatment'. Another explanation is that the rich countries refused their requests for a more adequate representation of their interests. This is why the areas in which they had comparative advantages – textiles, apparel, and agriculture – remained largely or completely outside the GATT framework and why their exports were subject to fewer and smaller tariff reductions than those from developed countries (Srinivasan 1999).

Whatever the relative historical merits of the first explanation, the developing countries submitted to a much greater degree of multilateral disciplines in the Uruguay Round. Thus, they insisted much less on special treatment, except for the highly technical new issues such as sanitary and phytosanitary standards, and intellectual property rights (TRIPS) where they were granted longer implementation periods (see Brewer and Young 1998, Chapter 10, for a fuller treatment). This reflects both their increased share in world trade and their membership size: almost four-fifths of WTO members are developing countries. So far, so good. It is the continued relevance of the second explanation that throws light on the misgivings of developing countries with the heritage of the Uruguay Round and the agenda for the new global trade round, aborted-at-launch in 1999 in Seattle and since subject to more or less energetic reanimation efforts by the rich countries.

The reasons why developing countries are unhappy with the legacy of the Uruguay Round are multiple. One, requirements resulting from implementing the provisions of the agreements in, respectively, services (GATS), investment (TRIMS), and TRIPS – the pet projects of the rich countries – are complicated and costly. Whether gains eventually will outweigh costs, is anyone's guess. Two, the legal firepower it would take to pursue cases successfully under the new Dispute Settlement Mechanism requires advanced

Markets and Authorities

information-gathering and analytical skills, along with deep pockets, that many delegations from poorer countries cannot afford. This also applies to their institutional capacities at home. Unlike the IMF and the World Bank, the WTO has only a very small secretariat, so most of the analysis of issues and development of positions is either done by member states in their capitals, or not at all (Michalopoulos 1999b). Some small and low-income members are so hard-pressed for resources that they cannot even afford a delegation in Geneva. Three, developing countries are suspicious of new issues the developed countries are pushing onto the agenda for a new round. They believe that the introduction of labour and environmental standards is mainly protectionism by other means. They distrust the EU's motives for bringing in competition policy as a vehicle to promote its firms' exports and to facilitate global mergers, and not to discipline market power of MNCs in foreign, including developing-country markets (Hoekman and Holmes 1999). As long as the WTO allows rich countries to promote export cartels, and rich-country firms to target developing-country exporters with anti-dumping suits, this fear makes a lot of sense. Last but not least, rich countries have not lived up to their side of the bargain – protectionism in textiles and clothing, leather goods, and agriculture is rampant.

Rich Country Market Access for Developing Country Industrial Products

Table 4.1 Rich Country Market Access for Industrial Products from Developing Countries

Countries	Textiles and clothing	Leather, footwear, etc.	All goods
(a) Share of duty-free tariff lines in bound tariffs			
Canada	6.5	22.5	34.5
US	11.3	28.1	39.4
EU	2.1	22.8	26.9
Australia	7.3	9.2	17.7
Japan	2.8	32.0	47.4
(b) Simple averages of bound tariffs			
Canada	12.4	7.6	5.2
US	8.9	8.4	3.9
EU	7.9	4.8	4.1
Australia	28.8	17.5	14.2
Japan	6.8	15.7	3.5

Table 4.1 continued

Countries	Textiles and Clothing	Leather, footwear, etc	All goods
(c) Standard deviation of bound tariffs (=dispersion)			
Canada	5.1	5.9	5.0
US	6.6	13.0	5.6
EU	3.2	5.0	4.0
Australia	17.8	13.4	14.7
Japan	2.7	20.1	6.0
(d) Share of tariff lines with duties above 15% (=tariff peaks)			
Canada	30.6	17.1	5.8
US	13.0	14.9	3.5
EU	0.0	11.2	1.5
Australia	73.3	37.2	25.3
Japan	0.3	39.0	1.8
(e) Simple average bound tariff by stage of processing (=tariff escalation)			
Canada			
raw materials	2.5	0.3	1.6
semi-manufact.	11.1	5.7	4.8
finished products	14.5	10.3	5.7
US			
raw materials	2.8	0.0	0.8
semi-manufact.	9.1	2.3	4.1
finished products	9.1	11.7	4.1
EU			
raw materials	2.6	0.1	5.1
semi-manufact.	6.6	2.4	4.0
finished products	9.7	7.0	4.0
Australia			
raw materials	1.5	4.2	1.5
semi-manufact.	22.9	11.5	12.3
finished products	35.7	22.0	16.7
Japan			
raw materials	2.6	0.1	2.2
semi-manufact.	5.9	10.4	4.0
finished products	8.3	20.7	3.4

Source: WTO (2001b)

In the give and take of the Uruguay Round developing countries achieved a commitment from the rich countries to ease substantially market access for those products in which they are competitive. Among industrial products, this means primarily textiles, clothing, and leather products. Hence, in an ideal post-Uruguay Round world, tariffs and non-tariff barriers (NTBs) would have become especially low for exactly these products. In reality, the exact opposite happened. This does not necessarily contravene the letter of WTO rules. But it makes a mockery of their spirit.

By virtually any indicator, rich countries have dragged their feet to opening up their markets to competition from producers in developing countries (see Table 4.1). First, the average share of duty-free tariff lines is extremely low for textiles, clothing, and leather products (a). (In fact, it is higher in all other product categories.) Second, the overall level of protection also remains especially high for these categories (b). For example, in Japan, post-Uruguay Round MFN rates for a pair of leather shoes valued at $25 will reach 160 per cent. Likewise, in North America, exports by least developed countries of textiles and leather products remain outside the scope of US and Canadian GSP (UNCTAD 2001). Courtesy of US textile manufacturers, labour unions, and the politicians they bankroll, LDC textile exports must use US-supplied fabrics to qualify for more liberal market access – not exactly an application of free trade principles. Third, tariff dispersion exists even within the relevant product categories (c). Since more uniform tariff rates are less likely to be highjacked by industrial lobbies who request protection, the opposite should be the case: the fewer tariff peaks and troughs, the better. Fourth, tariff peaks are highest for textiles and clothing, except in the EU and Japan, and for leather goods (d). Fifth, tariff escalation in the two categories is also rampant, even where – as in the EU and Japan – tariffs in general de-escalate (e). Since industrialization requires realising increasing levels of local value added, tariff escalation is an impediment to development.

The phasing out of NTBs has remained far behind the developing countries' expectations. The Uruguay Round Agreement on Textiles and Clothing (ATC) mandated the dismantling of the Multifibre Agreement (MFA), a network of bilateral quotas between the US, the EU, Norway, and Canada on the one hand, and 30 developing and transition economies on the other. Specifically, the ATC provided for the stepwise integration of this sector into WTO rules, fixing the share of textile and clothing imports to be liberalized and tariffied in four phases over ten years, namely 1995–2004. Table 4.2 shows that NTBs were still pervasive in the beginning of the second phase. What was supposed to happen afterwards was the elimination of quotas for integrated products and an enlargement of the remaining quotas. Importing members were given the discretion to decide which products to integrate first as long as they were drawn from the entire textile and clothing product range. They were entitled to invoke special safeguard mechanisms to enforce bilateral quotas for limited periods for products not yet integrated. This is what the agreement said in principle.

Table 4.2 Pervasiveness of Core Non-tariff Barriers in 1996 (% of tariff lines affected)

Country	Textiles and Clothing	Manufacturing
Canada	42.9	7.8
US	67.5	17.9
EU	75.2	13.4
Japan	31.9	10.3

Source: WTO (2001b)

In practice, the rich countries exploited the leeway they negotiated for themselves in the ATC. During the first two stages, until 1998, the 33 per cent of textiles and clothing imports brought under WTO rules were mostly low value-added products. They also included so-called unrestrained products. For example, if the US has always had quotas on a certain type of tops while Norway never did, Norway can still count the integration of this product toward the fulfilment of the ATC provisions. Again, this does not violate the letter of the agreement but clearly does not honour its spirit, either. Overall, the implementation of the agreement turns out to be backloaded. Most products that are actually or potentially important to developing countries will remain under the quota system until late 2004, when the MFA is supposed to end (WTO 2001b).

Table 4.3 Initiations of Anti-dumping Investigations by Sector, 1987–99

Product	(a) 1987–99	(b) 1995–99	% post–UR (=(b)/(a))
Textiles	217	97	45
Footwear	37	11	30
Leather	9	3	33
Total AD	2 812	1 218	43

Notes: UR = Uruguay Round

Source: WTO (2001b)

Finally, textiles, footwear, and leather continue to be prominent targets of anti-dumping suits. In fact, 30–45 per cent of all antidumping investigations initiated since 1987, the beginning of the Uruguay Round, fell into the half decade following its conclusion (see Table 4.3). In the same period, the developed countries directed 50 per cent of their investigations against developing countries. All of this goes a long way to explaining why developing countries are deluded by the implementation of the Uruguay Round accords.

Rich Country Market Access for Developing Country Agricultural Products

The preamble of the Uruguay Round Agreement on Agriculture promises the establishment of a fair and market-oriented agricultural trading system. Subjecting agricultural policies for the first time to multilateral rules and disciplines was meant to introduce more market orientation while acknowledging concerns about food security in developing countries and market disruption in developed countries. More specifically, the agreement targeted market access, domestic support, and export subsidies. The tariffication of NTBs and the opening of formerly closed markets intended to facilitate more and better market access. Domestic support programmes were brought under disciplines aimed at curbing trade distortions. And export subsidies were made subject to a schedule of gradual reduction with a view to final elimination.

This sounds better than it turned out. Rich-country markets remain difficult to penetrate; for commodities such as poultry meat or cheese the share of imports in total consumption is as low as 5 per cent, and there is hardly any difference between the first and the second half of the 1990s. Applied tariffs continue to be high, on average some four to five times as high as those on industrial products. Thirty-seven WTO members entertain almost 1 400 tariff quotas; the US and the EU alone hold 141. Of the total, only 560 are scheduled to increase over the implementation period of the Uruguay Round. These quotas often have low fill rates; in 1999, on average only about one half for most products. Tariff escalation makes it difficult for developing country exporters to gain a foothold in food processing industries (OECD 2001d, UNCTAD 2001, WTO 2001b,c).

The coffee trade is a case in point. Coffee is the world's most traded commodity in volume terms after crude oil. A long-term decline in coffee prices, with a two-thirds reduction since 1997 alone, along with increasing demand for high-quality beans in the most important markets, especially the US, means that the multinationals who control the bulk of the market – Sarah Lee, Nestlé, Procter & Gamble, and Philip Morris – have been having a field day. And that the small farmers in Guatemala or Ethiopia where coffee used to be a major revenue earner are having one bad day after another because they cannot make ends meet. They get only about 6 (rarely up to 20) per cent of the retail value, while roasters in consuming countries get 30 per cent. To see where the real profit goes, we need only visit our local coffee shop (cf. Amaral 2001).

If global poverty were not misgoverned, the small farmers in coffee producing countries would be afforded at least as high a chance as the multinationals to take advantage of liberalization. In case of the multinationals, the dismantling of the export quota agreement in 1989 meant that their supply conditions improved dramatically. In case of the producing countries, tariff escalation prevents them from capturing a larger share of the value added. In 2000, the US re-exported 10 per cent and the EU 28 per cent of the coffee beans they imported, half of which roasted and in soluble form. Table 4.4 shows that they engage in blatant import substitution. This does not just promote domestic industries. It also prolongs and exacerbates poverty elsewhere.

Table 4.4 Bound Tariffs on Coffee by Stage of Processing

Importer	Stage of processing	Bound rate	% tariff lines excl. from Ø
EU	unprocessed	3	0
	semi-processed	9	0
	prepared or preserved	10	79
US	unprocessed	0	0
	semi-processed	0	0
	prepared or preserved	2	55
Japan	unprocessed	8	0
	semi-processed	7	0
	prepared or preserved	20	0

Note: Ø = average (the more tariff lines excluded from the average bound tariff, the more protectionist the trade regime)

Source: WTO (2001b, Appendix Table III.1)

Non-traditional exports face anti-dumping and countervailing action, and health and sanitary regulations keep out imports of goods that are not in compliance. Sometimes it is bureaucratic idiocy that prevents effective market access. In a wonderful example of entrepreneurial success in one of the world's poorest countries, a Mauritanian woman set up a state-of-the-art camel dairy in Nouakchott, providing 800 Nomad families with an income. Since butter and milk production is uneconomical because of EU-subsidised dairy exports, she moved into cheese production. But although she found a German importer to take her entire output, none of her cheese made it into the EU – because of a lack of specific regulations concerning camels (James 2001). Special agricultural safeguards, though not much used so far, could be invoked to control imports perceived to be ruinous in terms of their volumes or their prices. North America and the EU alone have almost 900. Not surprising then that the developing country share of world merchandise exports roughly doubled in 1980–99, but grew by less than one-fifth for agricultural exports (OECD 2001c, UNCTAD 2001, WTO 2001a).

Table 4.5 EU Export Subsidies and Import Penetration

Product	Subsidised exports, % total exports, 1998	Import penetration rate, 1999
Beef	95	5.4
Butter	110	6.0
Cheese	70	2.3
Other milk products	82	-
Coarse grains	115	3.1
Eggs	83	-
Fruit & vegetables (fresh)	41	-
Fruit & vegetables (processed)	27	-
Pigmeat	62	0.3
Poultry meat	35	3.8
Rice	52	-
Skim milk powder	111	7.6
Sugar	30	12.6
Wheat/wheat flour	114	3.7

Notes:
(a)   Subsidized exports may exceed 100 per cent because of the use of previous-year allowances.
(b)   The import penetration rate measures the volume share of imports in total consumption.

Source: OECD (2001c, Annex Tables III.2, IV.2)

In 1999, OECD countries subsidized agriculture with a whopping $361 billion, about as much as Sub-Saharan Africa's GDP. 'Enough', as an African partner at McKinsey's quipped at the 2001 meeting of the World Economic Forum, 'to fly every cow in OECD countries around the world once each'. These subsidies are approximately twice the value of total agricultural imports from LDCs, and accounted for 40 per cent of the total value of OECD agricultural production, an increase from 31 per cent in 1997 due to lower world prices. Sugar, milk, dairy products, fruit and vegetables, rice, and meat are among the most highly subsidized products (OECD 2001a).

The rich countries mostly export semi-processed and processed goods to each other. In the late 1990s, they bought less than 10 per cent of their agricultural imports in developing countries. But the bulk of export subsidies is on commodities sold to developing countries. The EU subsidises 20 products (and accounts for 90 per cent of OECD subsidies) and the US 13. Both have overshot their annual export subsidy commitments for certain products by up to one half (OECD 2001a). For producers in poor countries there is effectively no level playing field. They compete against rich country, especially EU, exports that are offered at artificially low prices while their own exports are made artificially expensive (see Table 4.5). Small wonder that trade experts from developing countries find the one-sided liberalization agenda of the rich countries hypocritical (Turner 1999).

The Costs of Change

Globalization is about change. Change requires adaptation. Global adjustments could be collective, or governed. The misgoverned default solution will always favour the strong because the existing distribution of resources affords the strong the privilege of taking their time. This is the common thread that links the trends and stories of market access alluded to above.

Take the EU's early 2001 Everything-but-Arms initiative. It essentially extended immediate tariff- and duty-free access to all products from the world's least developed countries (LLDCs). Exceptions include remaining restrictions on bananas, rice, and sugar. They are scheduled gradually to be dismantled by 2006 and 2009, respectively (Council Regulation (EC) 2001). Since the LLDCs have negative balance sheets in pretty much all agricultural products, in general this initiative will not lead to much import displacement in the near future (cf. Hoekman et al. 2001). Import surges of more than 25 per cent of any given product in fact could trigger temporary suspensions of the agreement. Who pays the bill for adjustment? Perhaps the poor in sugar plantations in ACP countries such as Mauritius, Fiji, or Guyana because the former trade privileges of these countries are lifted in favour of yet poorer countries such as Malawi. It is surely not EU beet farmers who foot the bill. In May 2001 EU agricultural ministers decided to leave the subsidy system for sugar – with prices 2.6 times above world prices – largely unchanged until 2006.

The US treatment of LLDC textile producers is even worse. The 2000 African Growth and Opportunity Act provides a large number of Sub-Saharan African countries with duty- and quota-free access if they source fabrics and yarns from the US. By contrast, if African producers use locally produced yarns, they face restrictive quotas. In line with the OECD's 2001 agreement to untie aid, 'Tied Trade instead of Tied Aid' could have been the Clinton Administration's motto to propagate this. Whoever loses big time from this kind of liberalization, it is certainly not the producers or the workers in the US. It might seem curious that the rich countries claim long transition periods for opaque subsidy schemes with major distortionary effects on world markets while Caribbean banana producers – 70 per cent of whose revenue derive from banana exports – are allowed only a few years to figure out how fundamentally to redress their entire economic structure. But it is not curious. It merely reflects the rational use of power and influence substantially unmitigated by concerns to address poverty against producer-controlled farm ministries and other lobbies in the rich countries.

FREEDOM OF MOVEMENT FOR SOME BUT NOT FOR OTHERS

People who cannot make a living from selling what they make may be inclined to pack up and leave in search for better conditions. They become migrants, joining the approximate 2.5 per cent of the world population in 2000 whose residence is away from their country of origin for longer than one year (IOM/UN 2000). With the labour force in developing countries estimated to grow from 1.4 billion to 2.2 billion in 1995–2025, push factors of migration are set to stay (Stalker 2000). In theory, like free trade, immigration enhances welfare not just for the migrants but on average also in the host countries (Coppel et al. 2001, see also Glover et al. 2001). Reality is more complicated because societies are made up of individuals who are not interested in average gains but in their own, and who become concerned when they perceive to be losing something. If the real or imagined losers matter, politicians tend to protect them from outside competition. Thus on the whole the rich countries have reacted to increasing international mobility since the 1980s through reduced entry quotas. Multilateral cooperation, as with the EU's Schengen Accord, is often about the exclusion of migrants, rather than about maximizing the benefits of migration for source and host countries (Castles 1999, see also OECD 1999). The only people from developing countries whose migration is facilitated and encouraged both by national legislation in the rich countries and international accords such as the General Agreement on Trade in Services (GATS) are those with high skills in short supply, especially in the new economy. Ideally, their remittances and further skill upgrading abroad help the source countries, especially in case of eventual return migration. But source countries are also concerned about brain drain. The evidence as to which effect prevails is inconclusive (*International Migration* 1999).

International migration is not a neat affair. For a start, the majority of people leave their homes only because they see no other way to make ends meet. They don't hit the road because it's fun. In the absence of poverty or unemployment, they would rather stay where they are. In the receiving countries, they confront increasingly restrictive immigration regimes on the one hand, and a persistent demand for cheap labour – within agriculture, services, construction, and manufacturing – on the other (IOM/UN 2000). Because of the disjuncture of immigration policies and the informal labour market, an increasing number of migrants rely on traffickers to organize the trip from source to recipient country (IOM 1998). They may still be voluntary migrants. But they entrust their fate to the same international crime networks that are estimated to sell 700 000–2 000 000 women and children into (mostly sex) slavery each year (IOM/UN 2000). Thus they become subject to the same exploitative mechanism; the smuggling of migrants easily degenerates into trafficking. Just like girls and women from the world's poor regions are available to men in the rich countries for sex (e.g. IOM 1996), migrants generally are available to employers in rich countries for sweatshop labour. Trafficking exists because it is profitable for the traffickers and for those who avail themselves of the lower cost of illegal migrants (Morrison and Crosland 2001).

For the migrants themselves, it often means misery, alienation, exploitation, and even death. North Africans on their way to Spanish orchards risk drowning in their 'pateras' when crossing the Strait of Gibraltar. Together with their Ecuadorian colleagues they work long shifts for a fraction of the minimum wage and spend the night in inhumane and unsanitary living conditions. At the same time, they were instrumental in the spectacular development of greenhouse crops in Andalusia, traditionally one of the EU's poorest regions. Construction workers from Cape Verde help build hotels for the booming tourism industry on the Canary Islands. Tough luck when they become victims of work-related accidents; being illegal they do not enjoy the sort of protection and health insurance accorded to domestic workers (Natacha 2001). This is in part because the rich countries made commitments under the GATS primarily for intra-corporate transferees and business visitors. These commitments do not help those who scale the metal fence between Mexico and the US hoping to find construction or precision manufacturing jobs; NAFTA does not provide for the free movement of workers. Even when migrants from poor countries are legally employed, they are vulnerable. Filipino maids have been subjected to ill-treatment in Japan, and their wages have been withheld in Hong Kong (Blain 1998).

In sum, the rich countries are co-responsible for poverty in the developing world because they restrict market access for the goods of poor-country producers (cf. White 2001). They also make it hard for poor migrants legally to join the labour market of recipient countries. For those they manage to intercept, this means anything between extended stays in temporary centres and swift deportation. For those that make it, it often means a deprived, precarious, clandestine and at best second-class existence without minimal guarantees for human rights (reflected in the very poor ratification record of the 1990 UN Convention on Rights of Migrant Workers and Members of their Families). The last group thus remains poor, too, but in a rich country. This is hypocritical, and yet another example of the misgovernance of poverty.

SOME LIKE IT HOT – POLLUTION AND CLIMATE CHANGE

In the late 1990s, rich countries consumed roughly 40 million barrels of oil per day, about half of world primary demand. Generating $100 of income in the world's most advanced economies requires about 300kg of natural resources. This makes the G-8 countries responsible for almost half the global emissions of carbon dioxide. According to projections by the OECD, OECD countries are likely to increase greenhouse gas emissions by a third by 2020. This is because the reduction of energy intensity is more than compensated for by the increase in total energy use (OECD 2001b). Transatlantic disputes about how to deal with greenhouse gas emissions indicate that the US in particular feels it can afford to live without an international accord. No wonder – the primary victims of global warming do not live in Washington DC or anywhere else in North America. Instead, they live in water-stressed Northern Nigeria in ever closer proximity to the advancing desert. Or in Costa Rica where officials had hoped to combat deforestation by including forests in a climate change treaty. Or in Bangladesh or the small island states such as Pacific Kiribati where erratic weather patterns threaten devastation from flooding and an increased risk of drowning, diarrhoea and respiratory diseases, hunger, and malnutrition.

The list of projected adverse impacts of global warming does not make for soothing reading for anybody. But for the poor in the developing world, it reads like a horror story. Thus, according to the UN Intergovernmental Panel on Climate Change, it includes:

1. A general reduction in potential crop yields in most tropical and sub-tropical regions for most projected increases in temperature; [...]
2. Decreased water availability for populations in many water-scarce regions, particularly in the sub-tropics;
3. An increase in the number of people exposed to vector-borne diseases (e.g. malaria) and water-borne diseases (e.g. cholera) and an increase in heat stress mortality;
4. A widespread increase in the risk of flooding for many human settlements (tens of millions of inhabitants in settlements studied) from both increased heavy precipitation events and sea-level rise. (IPCC 2001, 4)

How well societies cope with climate change prominently depends on wealth, the technologies and infrastructure at their disposal, and on their management capabilities more generally. Put simply, most Kansans can turn up the air conditioner when they feel like it. Most Kenyans cannot. The least developed countries, where most of the world's poor live, have the lowest adaptive capacity but they are the worst affected and thus the most vulnerable. In fact, the scientists on the UN panel predicted, with medium confidence, that global warming would increase the disparity in well-being between rich and poor countries (IPCC 2001).

The IPPC also predicted that the emissions of developing countries would reach those of developed countries in 2015–20. Yet climate change is not the doing of poor, especially rural communities because their energy consumption at the global level is too marginal to matter. Therefore, they are not responsible for it. If the rich countries were serious about alleviating global poverty, they would do something about all the other pressures that afflict the poor. Seeing that drastic absolute reductions in greenhouse gas emissions are not in the cards, rich countries could reimburse developing countries for ecological initiatives such as the Mesoamerican Biological Corridor, a forest chain from Mexico through all Central American states to Panama. That would make environmental sense by cutting carbon dioxide emissions. And it would help the poor in those areas to reduce their vulnerability to the very climate change that the rich countries are thrusting upon them.

THE PROFILE OF A RACKET

How the global economy is run is a matter of human choice, so too is what to do about the world's poor. The OECD's target for development assistance is 0.7 per cent of rich-country GDP. Net aid disbursed fell from 0.33 to 0.24 per cent in 1987–98. UNCTAD urged a doubling of official aid to Sub-Saharan Africa over the next decade to kickstart private capital inflows via rising national savings and faster growth (UNCTAD 2000a). Nobody knows whether this would work. What is clear is that UNCTAD and OECD have distinctly different ideas about the sense, feasibility, and desirability of global redistribution (see also White 2001). Ultimately, this belongs in the realm of morality and is not an issue of governance.

The world's poor face a distinctly unlevel playing field in the global economy. Many of their products are unwelcome in the markets that matter most. If the poor stay put to sit out their fate, many of them face a future in which an increasingly hostile environment will make survival yet more difficult. If they heed the call of the rich countries' informal labour markets, they will lead illegal existences that only rarely allow the escape from poverty. What they are up against is not some anonymous market mechanism that marginalizes a certain part of humanity as the price for letting everybody else reap the fruits of globalization. Nor are they the victims of a global financial system run amok. Of course, financial crises affect the poor disproportionately; but it does not take a crisis for them to suffer their current fate. Instead, they are victims of misgovernance.

In the areas of direct relevance to the world's poor reviewed in this chapter – market access for industrial products, agricultural goods, workers, and greenhouse gas emissions – it is governments that make choices. They control tariffs, impose NTBs, finance export subsidies, police the borders, and tax pollution. It was also they who convinced developing countries to work with them in the Uruguay Round on an entirely new set of issues (for the latter) that led to economic reforms and made doing business in many emerging markets easier. So the problem of poverty does not exist because rich-country governments, on the retreat from markets worldwide, cannot get a handle on its underlying causes. The opposite is true: through their trade, labour market, and environmental policies, rich countries directly influence the extent and the depth of poverty. This is not a case of the *Retreat of the State* (Strange 1996). Instead, it is an – albeit no longer terribly successful – attempt by a group of rich states to advance globalization while minimizing adjustment costs at home at the expense of weaker participants in the system.

The liberalization of global product markets could mean very tough adjustments for apparel workers in the US or small dairy farmers in Switzerland. It does not, because their governments shield them from the winds of change. In principle, there is nothing wrong with that. Except that the way protection is afforded directly impacts on how the poor participate in, and benefit from, the global economy. The very same governments have no qualms about taking developing country offenders to task for real or alleged infringements of intellectual property rights or of the TRIMs agreement. Often, the result is more market power for rich-country firms. Hence, they are good at insisting on the fulfilment of issues of interest to them. They are also good at stalling on fulfiling issues of interest to developing countries. This is not the accidental outcome of an international development agenda that is complicated anyway and bedevilled by resource problems, design questions, and technical difficulties. It is a smart game played by those who can afford it and who so far have largely managed to get away with it. It is a game with the cards stacked in favour of the house – a rich-country racket.

A big financial service provider from an OECD country will always have more clout than a maize farmer in Africa. But the whole point of international economic cooperation between states is to introduce some degree of civility, in the form of rules and regulations, into running the world economy. That diminishes the relative throw weight of individual participants as in the law of the jungle. Stopford and Strange warned that the impacts on host countries of multinational firms (and their home-country governments) are too diverse to allow facile generalizations (1991). Yet one is in order: If rules are bad and regulations ignored (or misgoverned), the strong – countries, firms, or individuals – are more likely to have their way, and the weak, especially the poor, are more likely to suffer.

What introduces some elements of governance of poverty is other kinds of authorities, smartly playing the markets in the poors' favour. Under WTO legislation, South Africa's (or Brazil's) refusal to honour intellectual property rights of anti-retroviral drugs to fight HIV could have exposed the country to trade sanctions. Western governments always looked out for the patent privileges of the pharmaceutical industry, and the US government regularly put offending countries on its 301-watch list, making them eligible for trade sanctions. Yet the campaign started in February 2001 by Oxfam, the British charity, to discredit the pricing practices of multinational pharmaceutical companies in poor countries forced the latter to back down for fear of alienating their key client base in developed countries and of losing share value. Similarly, the investigation by the Global Alliance for Workers and Communities – a group composed of the International Youth Foundation, clothing MNCs Gap and Nike, the World Bank, plus universities and private foundations – into workplace practices of Nike suppliers in Indonesia, financed by Nike itself, found significant evidence of abuse, especially of female workers (Global Alliance for Workers and Communities 2001). The company promised to address the shortcomings and the Alliance is scheduled to return to study the effectiveness of the remedies after two years. In both cases, NGOs exerted the initial or the main pressure on other authorities (mainly firms and governments) with stakes in the issue. And in both cases the outcome was poor-friendly.

Public interest in corporate social responsibility can reduce poverty because it forces firms to take a hard look at how they trade, where they invest, and who they build supply networks with. Yet to address global poverty head on, means dismantling the racket. NGOs traditionally have not campaigned for market access. Debt forgiveness was a more prominent campaign theme, and there was guaranteed not to be any disagreements with potentially protectionist trade unionists. But market access would make for a good theme. Campaigners would not have to convince governments of the validity of their arguments, unlike with debt forgiveness. They would only need to remind rich-country governments of their obligations. Along with the fact that they, like the products of multinational firms, are a matter of human choice.

ACKNOWLEDGEMENT

I am grateful to Paolo Cecchini, Ron Dore, Valeria Fichera, Susan McEachern, and Ron Tiersky for comments, and to Zdenka Lomanova for research assistance.

REFERENCES

Amaral, Sergio (2001), 'Coffee's Bitter Taste: The Sector's Problems Will only Be Solved through Concerted Action by Producer and Consumer Countries', *Financial Times*, 17 May, http://globalarchive.ft.com/globalarchive/articles.html?id=0 10517001680&query=%22Coffee%27s+bitter+taste%22.

Binswanger, Hans P., and Joachim von Braun (1991), 'Technological Change and Commercialization in Agriculture', *World Bank Research Observer*, 6 (1), 57–80.

Blain, Didier (1998), 'Migrant Workers: Marissa's Choice', *Trade Union World*, 1 March, http://www.ainfos.ca/98/mar/ainfos00029.html

Brewer, Tom, and Stephen Young (1998), *The Multilateral Investment System and Multinational Enterprises*, Oxford: Oxford University Press.

Castles, Stephen (1999), 'International Migration and the Global Agenda: Reflections on the 1998 UN Technical Symposium', *International Migration* 37 (1), 5–19.

Chen, Shaohua and Martin Ravallion (2000), How Did the World's Poorest Fare in the 1990s?, Washington: World Bank, mimeo.

Cohen, Amon (1999), 'Caught in Capitalism's Crossfire', *Financial Times*, 6 December, 10.

Coppel, Jonathan, Jean-Christoph Dumont, and Ignazio Visco (2001), 'Trends in Immigration and Economic Consequences', *Economics Department Working Papers* no. 284, Paris: OECD.

Council Regulation (EC) No.416/2001 of 28 February 2001. (Everything but Arms) *Official Journal of the European Communities* L60/43–50.

Dolan, Catherine, John Humphrey, and Carla Harris-Pascal (1999), 'Horticulture Commodity Chains: The Impact of the UK Market on the African Fresh Vegetable Industry', Working Paper No. 96, Sussex: Institute for Development Studies.

Global Alliance for Workers and Communities (2001), 'Workers' Voices: An Interim Report on Workers' Needs and Aspirations in Nine Nike Contract Factories in Indonesia.', mimeo.

Glover, Stephen, Ceri Gott, Anaïs Loizillon, Jonathan Portes, Richard Price, Sarah Spencer, Vasinthi Srinivasan, and Carole Willis (2001), 'Migration: An Economic and Social Analysis', RDS Occasional Paper No. 67, London: Home Office.

Hoekman, Bernard, and Peter Holmes (1999), 'Competition Policy, Developing Countries and the WTO', *World Economy* 22 (6), 875–93.

Hoekman, Bernard, Francis Ng, and Marcelo Olarreaga. (2001), 'Tariff Peaks in the Quad and Least Developed Country Exports', Discussion Paper no. 2747, London: CEPR.

IFAD (2001), *Rural Poverty Report 2001*, Oxford: Oxford University Press.

International Migration 37. 1999. Special Issue on Migration and Development.

IOM (1996), *Trafficking in Women to Italy for Sexual Exploitation*, Geneva: IOM.

IOM (1998), 'Information Campaign against Trafficking in Women from Ukraine', Research Report, July, Geneva.

IOM/UN (2000), *World Migration Report*. (no place): UN.

IPCC (2001), 'Summary for Policymakers. Climate Change 2001: Impacts, Adaptation, and Vulnerability.' 19 February, mimeo.

James, Barry (2001), 'Africans' Camel Cheese Meets EU Bureaucracy. (Or How Poor Countries Try, and Fail, to Trade)', *International Herald Tribune*, 14 May, http://search.iht.com/search97cgi/s97_cgi?SiteVersion=DOM&Query=camel+chee se.

Lundberg, Matthias, and Lyn Squire (1999), 'The Simultaneous Evolution of Growth and Inequality', World Bank, mimeo.

Michalopoulos, Constantine (1999a), 'Developing Country Strategies for the Millennium Round', *Journal of World Trade* 33 (5), 1–30.

Michalopoulos, Constantine (1999b), 'The Developing Countries in the WTO', *World Economy* 22 (1), 117–43.

Milanovic, Branco (2002), 'True World Income Distribution, 1988 and 1993: First Calculation Based on Household Surveys Alone', *Economic Journal* 112 (January), 51-93.

Morrison, John, and Beth Crossland (2001), 'The Trafficking and Smuggling of Refugees: The End Game in European Asylum Policy?', Working Paper no. 39, Geneva: UNHCR.

Natacha, David (2001), 'Europe's Southern Gate', *Trade Union World*, 2 March, http://www.icftu.org/displaydocument.asp?Index=991212402&Language=EN

OECD (1999), 'Measures Undertaken to Prevent and Combat the Employment of Foreigners in an Irregular Situation in Certain OECD Member Countries', DEELSA/ELSA/MI(99)4, Paris.

OECD (2001a), *Agricultural Policies in OECD Countries,* Paris: OECD.

OECD (2001b), *OECD Environmental Outlook,* Paris: OECD.

OECD (2001c), *The Uruguay Round Agreement on Agriculture. An Evaluation of its Implementation in OECD Countries,* Paris: OECD.

OECD (2001d), *The Uruguay Round Agreement on Agriculture. The Policy Concerns of Emerging and Transition Economies,* Paris: OECD.

Oxfam/IDS (1999), 'Liberalisation and Poverty', mimeo.

Oxford English Dictionary, 2nd ed. 1989. Oxford: Clarendon Press.

Srinivasan, T.N. (1999), 'Developing Countries in the World Trading System: From GATT, 1947, to the Third Ministerial Meeting of WTO, 1999', *World Economy* 22 (8), 1047–68.

Stalker, Peter (2000), *Workers without Frontiers,* London: Lynne Rienner.

Stopford, John, and Susan Strange, with John Henley (1991), *Rival States, Rival Firms,* Cambridge: Cambridge University Press.

Strange, Susan (1996), *The Retreat of the State,* Cambridge: Cambridge University Press.

Thrupp, Lori Ann, with Gilles Bergeron and William F. Waters (1995), *Bittersweet Harvests for Global Supermarkets: Challenges in Latin America's Agricultural Export Boom,* Washington: WRI.

Turner, Mark (1999), 'Developing Countries Prepare to Dare to Challenge the Goliaths of World Trade', *Financial Times,* 19 November, 4.

UNCTAD (2000a), *Capital Flows and Growth in Africa,* Geneva: UN.

UNCTAD (2000b), *The Least Developed Countries. Part 1,* New York: UN.

UNCTAD (2000c), 'The Post-Uruguay Round Tariff Environment for Developing Country Exports: Tariff Peaks and Tariff Escalation', TD/B/COM.1/14/Rev.1, 28 January (UNCTAD/WTO joint study), Geneva.

UNCTAD (2001), 'Is there Effectively a Level Playing Field for Developing Country Exports?', *Policy Issues in International Trade and Commodities,* Study Series no. 1, February, Geneva.

UNICEF (2001), *The State of the World's Children,* New York: UNICEF.

USTR (2000), *African Growth and Opportunity Act Implementation Guide,* Washington DC.

White, Howard (2001), 'National and International Redistribution as Tools for Poverty Reduction', Sussex: IDS, mimeo.

WHO (2000), *World Health Report 2000,* Geneva: WHO.

Winters, L. Alan (2001), 'Trade and Poverty: Is there a Connection?', Special Studies no. 5, Geneva: WTO.

WTO (2001a), 'Agricultural Trade Performance by Developing Countries 1990–99', G/AG/NG/S/6/Rev.1, Geneva, mimeo.

WTO (2001b), 'Market Access: Unfinished Business', Special Studies 6, Geneva.

WTO (2001c), 'WTO Agricultural Negotiations. The Issues, and where We Are now', Geneva, mimeo.

5. Pensioners to the Casino

Ronald Dore

GLOBALIZATION AND THE POSSIBILITY OF NATIONAL OPT-OUTS

It is a pity that we shall never know what caustic things Susan Strange might have had to say about the demonstrators in Seattle and Prague who see globalization as fundamentally the work of the devil – or about the solemn speeches which international bankers, when the police escorts finally get them to their meetings, have lately come to make about their heartfelt concerns for world poverty. She had no lack of sensitivity to the suffering of poor people: see the comments on debt relief in her last book. But she was too much of a cosmopolitan, and got too much fun out of teasing the rich and powerful to wish them out of existence. Globalization as a merging of peoples and cultures and a diffusion of political power did not much bother her in itself: what she wanted to warn us about was the possibility that the whole anarchic structure might come down about our ears, with the consequence that, as in the 1930s, the innocent poor would suffer for the sins and follies of our unelected bankers. She would have viewed America's downward slide in 2001 with a mixture of *schadenfreude* and concern.

Nevertheless, the combination of trade union protectionists, passionate environmentalists, third world sympathisers, and miscellaneous antinomian activists for whom 'globalization' has replaced 'capitalism' and 'the multinationals' as the central focus of indignation and hatred, may prove not to be a force to be dismissed lightly. Well before they were joined by the MacDonalds-trashers on the streets of Seattle, an internet-mobilized coalition of thoughtful rich-world campaigners had played a not inconsiderable part in mobilizing developing country opposition to the OECD's proposed Multilateral Investment Agreement.[1] And there was obvious justice in their argument – that 'national treatment' for foreign investors may seem like an enlightened application of the 'level playing field' principle of fairness and mutuality, but, as in rugby, it is also a recipe for making sure that the heavyweights win. They win, of course, because they are the best team, but 'best' only in the single dimension of point-scoring capacity. The losers may be more beautiful or have superior morals. They may be happier at home than on the pitch; they may be more artistically creative, more sensitive in personal relations, more loyal, more altruistic.

The thing about the global economy – or rather about the combination of free capital flows and the elevation to categorical imperative of the principle of free competition in the global economy – is that it is not like a game of rugby. In three respects. First, it is very hard to opt out of playing it, or to argue that golf, with its handicapping system, would be a better game to play; the heavyweights can apply formidable sanctions against anyone who tries to drop out. Second, the act of playing it may do something to all those other moral, aesthetic and social characteristics which you cherish and which you think favourably distinguishes you from the heavyweights. And third, umpires are weak, the rules are tenuous and easily over-ridden by mere muscle, and there is the danger of every game turning into a *sauve-qui-peut melée*.

Translated into less allegorical terms: (1) trade dependency is real dependency; (2) economic systems are embedded in societies with distinctive values to which their citizens may be attached; they may not want to give up their 'type of capitalism' and (3) both considerations interact with the Susan Strange problem of casino-like instability.

She was sceptical in her last book about the prospects of genuinely international institutions that could tame the anarchy of financial markets. She was also disinclined to accept that, as Ethan Kapstein argued, a good international agreement among sovereign governments, which sorted out who had to regulate whom, ought to be quite enough to make the system safe. She quoted, as she had in her previous book, Fred Hirsch and Jacques Polak, concluding that 'the only way out' was to reverse the whole process of globalization of financial markets with the reimposition of capital controls and the reassertion of national sovereignty. Enough economic pain, she said, and even that might be tried. But, she went on, given modern communications technology would it be feasible?

On the technology point, who knows? Missile technology breeds missile defence technology; Internet technology is breeding Internet control technology; financial transaction technology can breed the technology for monitoring financial transactions. On that point ignorance forces me into agnosticism.

The point of the present chapter is to ruminate on the other half of what I shall call the 'national opt-out possibility question' – not the 'can' but the 'want to'. Is the realistic prospect of efforts to recover national economic sovereignty just a question of suffering enough economic pain? If so, whose pain? How mobilized and translated into political action? Does there need also to be a background of non-economic pain – of a sense that globalization is hurting the nation in its values and way of life? And what might be the shape and the strength of the sort of political coalition that feels both the economic and the non-economic pain sharply enough to go for some form of national opt-out?

Answers to this enormous question can only be tentatively offered for one country at a time. As Pauly suggests in his paper, a Canadian national opt-out is not impossible to imagine, only implausible. This paper is about Japan, where both geography and culture considerably reduce the implausibility. Though that, again, depends on the degree of opt-out one envisages. There are many stages short of the escape to autarky of the 1930s though that seemed to be what Greenspan had in mind when he opined, in October 2000, that 'antipathy to globalisation runs so deep that a recession could force a retreat from market-oriented policies and a return to protectionism, even in the United States' (International Herald Tribune, 2 October 2000). But it is not impossible to imagine Japan, reversing its Big Bang, and stalling on the financial services liberalization negotiations left over from the Uruguay Round, while continuing full cooperation in free trade in goods, and other services.

This paper considers one aspect of the possibility of some such, albeit limited, opt-out, namely the effect that changes in Japan's pension system might have on the Japanese state's power to make such a change, and the willingness to do so of those who determine its policies. The effect on that power is, as in the Pauly scheme of things, via its effect on the state's legitimate authority. Changes in the pension system, and thereby in the constellation of voter interests and the likely nature of political coalitions, can have the long-run effect, both of weakening the state's authority in general, and its power to adopt opt-out policies in particular.

FINANCE: THE SPEARHEAD OF CULTURAL GLOBALIZATION

There can be little doubt about the processes – shall we call them Darwinian? – by which Big Bang-type openings of financial sectors to international competition change, not just financial transactions, but also the assumptions and expectations – and values – under, with and for which they are conducted. A former participant describes the process by which the heavyweight American investment banks cleaned out the City of London.

The gifted amateur has given way to the dynamic investment banker. The day starts at 7 a.m., not 9 a.m., 70 per cent of analysts work 70 hours per week and designer water has replaced the boozy lunch...Firms that employed a few hundred now employ thousands, spread across the world, and are often themselves part of even bigger enterprises ... . Personal relationships are different. The partnerships and family companies that dominated the City in the 1980s built up strong bonds with their employees. All things being equal, partners and staff were loyal for life, but frequent changes in ownership and the imposition of regular redundancies on the one side and the lure of the head-hunters'gold on the other have eroded these bonds. Loyalty has been replaced by commitment – while the relationship lasts.[2]

Americans were a major disrupting feature in the labour market in these years. The standard approach was to employ head-hunters and to plunder the 'marzipan layer' of the broking firms. The marzipan layer – below the icing but above the cake – was the senior executives of the broking and jobbing firms just below partnership level ... . This was an exciting and glamorous period for the marzipan level ... we were wanted, we were courted, enormous amounts of money were thrown our way.[3]

Bonds used to exist between firms as well as within firms but these have not survived.

One may not be much inclined to mourn the passing of the complacent old-boy culture of the City's long-established brokers and bankers. They inhabited an island of security and privilege in a society where the wealth-creators in agriculture and manufacturing were fully and often mercilessly exposed to the insecurities of the market.

But if one were a Japanese, one might feel differently about a society in which the principles on which the City once worked have become the general norm for whole swathes of the corporate manufacturing and service sector. For that is indeed one of the crucial characteristics of the Japanese version of what Michel Albert has taught us to call 'Rhenish' capitalism. It was all there in the 'Japanese' City: the security of lifetime career employment, loyalty (of the sort which precluded a NatWest banker from ever shifting to rival Barclays), bonds of obligation built up in long-term trading relationships between firms, and – the 'gentlemanly bit' – an acknowledgement that competitors are constrained to abide by the norms of a common culture in the maintenance of which their industry's material interest is vested. Japan, in other words, has generalized at a society-wide level the practice of relational, as opposed to arms-length trading – in the labour market with its career, not job, contracts; in the equity market with stable shareholdings (which prevented takeovers and made it possible to have corporations which could honour the lifetime employment guarantee at the expense of profits) and in intermediate goods markets where suppliers were treated as 'family'.

But now? The dominant ideology of Japan in the year 2000 – reflected in a series of reports commissioned by successive prime ministers – says that all those characteristics are little more than signs of backwardness, habits possible for Japan during its past period of high growth, but hopelessly damaging for a nation which confronts the problems of an ageing population, and the need to be open to the megacompetition of an ever more global economy. There is, to be sure, a fringe opposition which defends the status quo, or selected parts of it. It is animated by a mixture of a diffuse attachment to traditional Japaneseness, and nationalistic anti-Americanism, with a more explicit and principled dislike of over-ruthless competition, springing from attachment to the values of personal relations and the ethic of dutiful obligation which over-single-minded competition can destroy.

That articulate opposition is very much in a minority, but even among the reformers it has secret sympathisers. The reformers, indeed, divide fairly clearly into two groups. There are the, generally young, gung-ho enthusiasts in finance and the media, especially the economists with American PhDs who increasingly predominate in university economics departments, and the growing army of American MBAs in business and consultancy. But there are also the reluctant dutiful reformers who feel that – unfortunately – there is no other line for a patriotic Japanese to take. It is with 'loyal reluctance' that they go along with the Americanization programme. They do so in much the same spirit, it is a nice irony to reflect, as many of their grandfathers did when, by November 1941, they saw no other honourable course for Japan than to challenge America in a war no sensible person could see a hope of winning.

And once again their misgivings are basically that, if they do decide to play rugby, they will lose. One of the pitches on which the game is played, as in Britain, is in the competition for talent between foreign firms operating American or European personnel systems and Japanese firms. The Bank of Japan still manages to recruit the brightest of the bright from the best universities, but its senior officials are worried by the large numbers of their high flyers who are leaving after a few years spent learning the job, lured into foreign, largely American, firms with the offer of salaries twice or three times what the Bank would eventually pay them in their late 40s.

So this paper is about Japan. Specifically it is about what one can learn concerning the implications for possible opt-out decisions, from the current Japanese debates over what to do about pensions.

PENSIONS

But before getting to Japan, a word or two about pensions – pensions and ageing, pensions and the state, pensions and the finance industry, pensions and the Strange Casino.

First a mini-glossary. Of the major cross-cutting dimensions of variation in pension schemes, three seem to me important – the funded/pay-as-you-go divide, the state-market divide, and the individualist-collectivist divide.

Funded means that contributions towards pensions are built up in a fund which is kept separate from the current operations of the organizing entity (the state or a private corporation), the fund being invested and the pensions being paid from the yield of the investment. By contrast, in pay-as-you-go the fund may be notional or of minimal proportions, and the pensions paid out of current income – in the case of state schemes, the current contributions of those who look forward to pensions in the future. Although the term 'pay-as-you-go' is generally used only about state schemes, corporate pensions – in Germany, for example – may be essentially similar (the surplus of contribution income over current pension payments is available to the corporation as capital). The expectation on the part of present contributors to pay-as-you-go schemes that they will eventually get their pensions depends on the long-term viability of the organizing entity. This is usually thought to be more problematic in the case of corporations than in that of states. Hence there is an insurance scheme in Germany to deal with the possibility of the firm's bankruptcy, but no international insurance scheme for states, unless it be, ultimately, the IMF.

A funded system can be a defined benefit system (the corporation takes the risk of investment returns being lower than expected so that it may have to top up the fund to pay the benefits that have been guaranteed). Most corporate pensions still are of this kind in most countries, though fast diminishingly so in the US and the UK, especially for smaller firms. The alternative is a defined contribution system, 'defined contribution' being clever finance industry jargon for 'undefined benefit'; that is to say, contributors take the risk because their pensions depend on the actual eventual earnings of the investments into which their money has been put.

State/market has a triple significance. The obvious one is whether the pension scheme is run by a public authority or by a private entity – a corporation, a non-profit-making trust, or a profit-making financial firm. The second is whether or not the operations of private pension-providers are (a) facilitated by tax-exemption of the contributions or of the investment earnings of the fund, and (b) regulated to provide some measure of saver-protection. In practice they are nearly always both. The third is whether, if the state does build up a significant fund, that fund is invested by market criteria to maximize returns, or used also, at lower rates of return, for social infrastructure investment, justified on the basis of a social cost-benefit analysis. The vast housing projects funded by the Singapore Provident Fund are a famous example. So widely diffused have marketist assumptions become in pension discussions that even 'left-wing' international organizations such as the ILO refer to the possibility that governments will use funds this way as 'political risk'.

As for the collectivist-individualist dimension, all pension schemes involve some form of social pooling of personal risk – those who die young subsidize those who linger on. (A branch of insurance relatively free from moral hazard: pensions are thought to add little to the incentives to avoid death.) Nearly all state schemes divide into what is usually known as the first tier – a flat-rate basic pension, and an earnings-related second tier. The most collectivist forms are those where the first tier basic pension is universal and financed directly out of taxes – i.e., not dependent on contributions – as in Denmark, Finland, Iceland, Norway, Sweden, Canada, New Zealand (not quite universal in Australia where it is subject to a means test).[4] Moving along the collectivist-individualist spectrum, next come the compulsory-contribution schemes for a flat-rate basic pension (with penal or reduced-pension sanctions – or both – to reinforce the compulsion), then compulsory participation in earnings-related schemes involving some element of income-redistribution among income classes, and next compulsory schemes with no such redistribution (both usually confined to employees, with alternative schemes for the self-employed). The most individualistic of all are the voluntary defined-contribution schemes with tax-exemption provisions which can be of a highly regressive kind.

THE CONVENTIONAL REFORM WISDOM

There is quite a large economics literature on the implications of different pension schemes, much of it hostile to any form of pay-as-you-go system. 'As is well-documented in the literature, increases in pay-as-you-go social security will crowd out capital formation, which in turn will cause pretax wages to fall, interest rates to rise, and ultimately output to fall' says one author, who has calculated a general equilibrium model based on a stylized US economy which predicts that 'eliminating social security will increase steady-state capital by 22.8 percent, aggregate output by 9.8 percent, aggregate consumption by 5.2 percent and aggregate labour by 3.1 percent.'[5]

And if pay-as-you-go is this bad even in a general equilibrium model which calculates the nature of some chimerical stable state, then, says your standard neoclassical economist, the dynamics of ageing make it worse. A survey of the literature on the effects of ageing by the OECD[6] makes it clear that most studies view the policy problem as being the following. Since according to the lifetime cycle theory the working young save and the old spend, ageing means that savings will decline. Investment must also decline and so also does the rate of growth, and with the rate of growth so, also, the rate of return on investments, thus further discouraging savings, all of which is bad news both for the workers and the retired of future generations.

However, some of the assumptions of these projections are at least questionable. The younger affluent old also save. It may be rational to save more the higher rates of return become, but if you want to see a backward-sloping supply curve of savings persisting for years, you have only to look at Japan in the last decade. The assumption made in many of these models of a fixed production function linking investment rates (in physical capital, remember) and productivity growth rates, is pretty obviously questionable. (It would be interesting to know how many of the economists who make it are simultaneously gung-ho believers in the New Economy.)

The prescription, implicit or explicit, of much of this literature, is that pay-as-you-go schemes should be whittled down to a social safety-net minimum and funded systems substituted. It is reinforced by the argument that maintenance of pay-as-you-go with an ageing population requires increases in contribution rates that are politically impossible. This is so widely accepted as common wisdom, that Merrill Lynch can produce a paper on 'pension reform' with a league table which separates the laudable reformers from the laggard countries and base its measurements almost entirely on the extent to which state involvement in supporting the aged has been reduced.[7]

A Savings Glut?

What is rarely discussed, however, (by economists, let alone the Merrill Lynches who look forward to the extra investment management business) is the possibility that if the prescription were followed in all the advanced industrial societies, the so-called serious savings deficit might turn into a serious savings glut. Already, pension fund assets in the US, the UK and Holland hover, depending on the health of the equity and bond markets, around 100 per cent of GNP. This does not include the funds resulting from tax-exempt savings schemes which serve as individually managed pensions schemes, particularly for the self-employed, but are merged into general mutual funds.

Some enterprising statistician might like to calculate the annual flow of new savings which would result if all the OECD countries were to grow pensions funds to the same scale and in the same time frame (about two decades) as the pioneer countries, and if the universal concern with 'national competitiveness' were to prompt all countries to follow the pioneers in relaxing their traditional rules of prudential fund management in order to encourage investment in equities. Wonderful, say some. It is 'widely recognised that the growth of the new economy has been made possible by the existence and growth of large pools of risk capital mediated by the Anglo-

American financial services industry'.[8] So if we all had funded pensions we could all have a new economy, not just the Americans.

The trouble with pools is that they can evaporate, as the Nasdaq enthusiasts have been discovering since the turn of the century. The Japanese bubble (fed as much by Anglo-American funds as by Japanese corporation finance managers), the massive financial flow to and massive retreat from Asia which plunged their economies into chaos in 1997, and now the unfolding drama of the pricking of the Wall Street bubble, all look like signs of an already excess supply of liquidity. The nature of the business cycle has been changed, suggested *The Economist* recently. Now it is not triggered by interest rate rises to choke off inflation, and prolonged by swollen inventories, but by a lowering of earnings expectations caused by excessive investment prompted by cheap equity and the irrational exuberance induced by soaring stock prices. The resultant overhang of excess capacity and the indebtedness that produced it, may cripple the real economy for many years thereafter.[9] The question relevant to the present argument is how much that excess investment was produced by new savings and how much by credit creation.

One can also look at the savings glut argument from the bottom up – from the household income point of view. Profits, interest and rent, in most economies are largely absorbed by the corporate sector and used for reinvestment or to enhance balance sheets. As a proportion of household income,[10] even in Britain (1998–99, most pension funds are still building) they contribute 4 per cent directly and 7 per cent via pensions and annuities (though a small part of that 7 per cent may derive from unfunded company pensions, not from capital income of a pension fund). If household income is around 65 per cent of GNP, this 11 per cent of total household income represents about 7 per cent of GNP, all but half a per cent of which goes to retired households.

For those retired households in Britain, capital income amounts to 40 per cent and social security 50 per cent of their total receipts. (In a highly skewed distribution, of course, nearly 50 per cent of pensioners have financial assets worth less than £1500.[11]) Now assume that over the next 30 years, the ratio of the per capita income of pensioners to that of the working-age population is unchanged, but that two other things change: first, retired households grow from 25 per cent to 32 per cent of the total (well within the range of projections). Second, that pension income derived from profit, interest and rent earned by pensions funds, replaces three-quarters of the present social security payments (i.e. 37.5 per cent of the total household income of the retired) leaving only 12.5 per cent as a residual means-tested income-support safety net. Simple arithmetic shows that this would require the flow of capital income to households, at present 7 per cent of GNP, to grow to 16 per cent, assuming an unchanged ratio of 65 per cent household income to GNP.

In other words, there would have to be a big shift in the relative earnings of labour and capital. A sizeable amount – on the assumptions stated 9 per cent – of GNP would have to be shaved off the former, and added to the latter. And this at a time, we are constantly told, when human capital (normally rewarded with wages and salaries) is becoming vastly more important for the efficient functioning of the economy than the material capital which earns dividends interest and rent. (And insofar as labour too comes to be rewarded with profit shares and stock options, this only increases the needed shift further beyond that 9 per cent.)

The only way this could happen throughout an OECD world which decided to fund all its pensions in full would be through such a vast transfer of capital to the non-OECD countries and such greatly higher returns to those overseas than to domestic investments that the factor shares in GDP remain at a plausible level and only the shares in GNP change – all highly improbable.[12] It is equally improbable that some new 'New Economy' will contrive to price factors in some way irrelevant to their relative scarcity, thus turning the whole of economic wisdom upside down.

Not to labour the point further, the advocates of funded pensions who work out models of the future on the assumption that the real interest rate and the equity premium will be the same in the next 40 years as in the last 40 years (one such Merrill Lynch model assumes a 4 per cent constant real interest rate[13]) and urge every country to 'reform' their pensions, are promising an impossibility. If their advice is accepted, and interest rates manifestly fall, they will doubtless, on the basis of revised models, advise that people have to save more to reach their target earnings replacement rate – and so be even more certain to produce the stagnation that has afflicted Japan in recent years. Conventional wisdom must surely by then turn against them, and reassess the benefits of pensions paid, as-you-go, by a redistribution of labour income, with the revenue perhaps raised rather less in the form of payroll taxes than at present.

Equity: Inter- and Intra-Generational

Before leaving the pension question in general, there is one further equity issue which is made much of by some Japanese pension reformers, and hence plays a part in the political legitimacy debate. It has given rise to a sizeable body of literature over the last decade under the rubric of 'generational accounting'. It involves a lot of very clever econometrics and the November 2000 issue of the *Economic Journal* devotes its two lead papers to the topic. One of the literature's major policy concerns is, to put it in the words of one of those papers,[14] how can one 'produce a generational balance – a situation in which future generations face the same fiscal burden as the current generations when adjusted for growth (when measured as a proportion of lifetime earnings)?' Two, not-so-youthful Japanese economists calculate – and perceive it a gross injustice – that the generation born in 1935 will take out in pensions half a million dollars more than it contributed, while if contribution and benefit schedules remain unchanged, the cohort born in 2000 will receive a quarter of a million dollars less than its contributions[15] – a natural consequence of a pay-as-you-go system in a society with initially very high and subsequently decelerating income growth.

I suppose one ought to be glad to find economists who are interested in equality, but concentration on this form of inequality seems to me misplaced. Personally I am very fond of my grandchildren, but the least of the things about their futures that worries me is that, in order to have pensions comparable to mine they might end up with a proportionately larger fiscal burden than I have suffered. They will, even post-tax, probably have a larger income to start with, and in any case they will be enjoying all the public goods, the social infrastructure of hospitals and museums and transport facilities which were not there when I was a child. I see their welfare as depending much more on the way in which our choice of pensions systems affects *intra*generational equality in their future. I would like to see them able to live in a decently peaceful, open society where there is enough social solidarity to sustain decent health services and schools and public broadcasting, not in a society with wide income disparities where the lucky live in guarded compounds with razor wire and electronic surveillance systems to protect them and the unlucky have to take their chance of being burgled or mugged in the undefended areas outside.

The reader can hardly fail to have detected my own preference for maintaining a pay-as-you-go rather than a funded system. This is largely because there is more collective pooling of risks and more scope for redistribution in a pay-as-you-go system and consequently it is likely better to sustain social solidarity. It is also because I prefer a society in which gambling is marginalized to occasional 'flutters' as a form of entertainment, not obligatory for anyone who wants an income in old age, and dressed up by the dominant ideology as skilled asset management. That latter preference has been reinforced by personal experience of helping younger people to choose the British version of defined contribution schemes, the Personal Equity Plans, now renamed by the Labour government as Individual Savings Accounts. Anyone who gets that close to it discovers that market competition among providers translates into vast advertising expenditure, confusing claims which preclude any other rational choice than saving time by sticking in a pin, and the creaming off, by providers, of high administration costs and up-front charges: assymetrical information and assymetrical hype as well as the symmetrical ignorance that marks all forms of gambling.

All very well, say the proponents of funded systems, but the contribution rates to maintain a pay-as-you-go system will be prohibitive. It is hard to see why that should be so. Assume a growth rate of 1.5 per cent p.a. – of the order that Japan maintained during its 'lost decade' of the 1990s. Assume that the income of the increasing numbers of old people is maintained at, say, one half average post-tax earnings. The annual increase in the necessary transfer to the growing numbers of old people would not be more than 0.25 per cent for hardly any country over the next 30 years. Which leaves the 'impossibly burdened' working population still with an annual 1.25 per cent income increase.

In any case, the old of 2040 are going to get their income from the working population of 2040. (Short, as noted above, of large volumes of highly productive investment overseas.) The choice we face is between making the transfer through financial markets and financial claims, or through the political process.

Pensions and the Strange Casino

The first sense in which 'pension reform' relates to the stability of the international finance system is obvious. The growth of pension funds in the US and the UK, and the relaxation of their prudential rules encouraging the growth of an 'enterprise culture' by channelling more of the funds into equities has added to the stock of liquid mobile capital and hence to the risks of Gadarene over-shooting. If the rest of the OECD move in the same direction, scared by all the economic analyses which predict that ageing populations make pay-as-you-go pensions systems unsustainable and that a switch to funded systems is essential, the problem of a world awash with liquidity can only be exacerbated.

The switch to a funded system, when it happens, is almost certainly likely to be, (as in the tax-privileged American, so-called 401k, voluntary schemes or in the Chilean, or the new Swedish or the prospective British stakeholder schemes), of defined contribution form, organized through private providers on the basis of individual accounts. This has predictable effects on the possibility of a national opt-out. It shifts one more bit of the economy from state to market, thus whittling down the state's ability to control the economy. It removes one important area of collective action, one important base of the social solidarity which is a precondition for building a coalition in favour of a national opt-out. And, more specifically, it creates a large voting constituency of people who have a direct stake in global financial markets, a constituency in which people's stake is proportionate to their affluence, hence probably to their articulacy and their influence.

THE JAPANESE 'TYPE OF CAPITALISM' AND PENSIONS

I characterized Japan earlier as a society which had generalized to a society-wide level, the preference for relational as opposed to arm's length trading – in its employment system, its stable shareholding system, its supply chain relationships, etc. The attitudes and values built into its economic institutions are relevant to pensions issues in several ways. First is the high value placed on security and predictability; the security of fixed interest modes of saving, the security of established relationships, the security of personal trust as opposed to institutional trust in the judicial enforcement of contracts. Put in economists' terms, risk-adversity. Second, an acceptance of group constraints on individual self-assertiveness and self-interest maximization, whether the group is the company one works for or the industry or trade association or the nation. The third point concerns the nation as the relevant constraint-imposing group. There is a greater willingness than in most countries, certainly than in Britain or the US, to accept high top rates of income tax and inheritance taxes, or social security contributions or administrative guidance (if you are a wealthy whisky oligopolist to leave sake-brewing to the labour-intensive small firms, for instance), and a large measure of acceptance of the legitimacy of the state and of the officials who run it.

One can argue about the ingredients that go into this acceptance – how far it is traditional deference to authority: in the contemptuous words of a leading member of the American Chamber of Commerce 'they just can't shake off the old lord and peasant mentality', how far it is a product of the racial and cultural homogeneity of the Japanese population and the solidarity produced by their shared century and a half's experience of trying to gain for Japan a position of equality with the leading Western powers.

But at least partly it is a product of Japan's success in creating a meritocratic civil service with an elite ethos which, for all its occasional arrogance, does care about the 'national interest', and makes it clear in its distributional policies (like the segmentation of drinks markets mentioned above) that its concept of 'the nation' whose interest it serves is an inclusive one, and that they are not merely the tools of the rich and powerful. It may be, as the rational choice school would argue, that they would not sustain that concern for inclusiveness if they did not have to work through a legislature still dominated by politicians who rely for their votes on farmers and small-business men. Changes in class structure and voting banks may be a crucial factor behind the recent shift in the ideological climate, but these shifts take time to work through into policy.

At any rate, for the moment, and still after a decade of 'bureaucrat-bashing' as the officials themselves wryly describe it, (particularly directed at the Ministry of Finance which had one or two genuinely corrupt characters) this sense of the state's legitimacy is a factor to be taken account of. It contrasts sharply with the hostility towards the state which has always been endemic in those Anglo-Saxon countries where constitutional democracy was not, as in Japan, granted from above by benevolent rulers, but won through painful revolutionary struggles against tyrants, and where, in the last two decades, that hostility to the state has been theorized and philosophized in a dominant neoliberal ideology.

THE REFORM DECADE

The ambiguities of the reform movement in Japan have already been dwelt on. There are many genuine individualistic converts to the American way of life, but there are many more who support reform on the basis of a simple syllogism. America is booming, Japan is stagnating. America has highly competitive markets, minimal government controls and labour protection, corporations dedicated to maximizing shareholder value. Japan has none of those things. If Japan were to change so as to become like America, then it too would boom.

The actual institutional changes have not matched the reform rhetoric. Restructuring of firms usually involves voluntary early retirement, not dismissals. Wage systems have been modified to give more emphasis to performance and less to seniority, but only marginally. The scope for part-time contract working has been somewhat widened. Managers do seem to be giving more attention to their share price. Managerial stock options have been introduced in a relatively low-key way. Deregulation has intensified competition in a number of non-internationally-traded sectors – gasoline distribution, domestic air travel and retailing.

And Pensions

They may not yet have accomplished very much, but the intentions and the ideology of the reformers is clear. Certain key justifying phrases recur in their writings – competition, consumer sovereignty, the expansion of choice, but two are most important for present purposes. The first is 'fair differentials' (*kosei na rakusa*) (a phrase which frequently occurs in conjunction with the assertion that Japanese society has hitherto misconstrued the true meaning of equality: it is not equality of outcomes that counts, but equality of opportunity). The second is 'taking individual responsibility' (*jiko sekinin*) (this is still a dutiful culture, hence more emphasis on the responsibility of choosing rather than the liberating effects of expanded choice). Related recurring phrases are 'risk-taking' and 'the transformation of security-conscious savers into dynamic investors'.

What this means in terms of pension systems is clear, and adherents of the new ideology have not been slow to propose solutions to the ageing population problem: much less state, much more market: a whittling down of the public pension system and full-steam ahead for tax-privileged defined contribution, individual-account pensions. The debate has acquired headline prominence, partly because the Japanese intelligentsia has long had a taste for long-term forecasting, and partly because the ageing of the post-war baby boomers means a more dramatic transformation of the demographic pyramid than other countries face.

A word first about what Japan's current pension arrangements are. The basic pension pays some $600 a month (at current exchange rates: perhaps a little under $500 at purchasing power parity) For the earlier generations after the scheme's introduction benefits were paid out of general taxation, but for later cohorts, the right to the pension depends on contributions which are compulsory, though, since costly exhortation is the only means used for enforcement, 'delinquents' – mostly part-time and temporary workers but including also many well-off, self-employed, self-insured free-lance professionals – abound. By some estimates, they amount to over 40 per cent of those who are neither employees (whose contribution is deducted at source) or given a low-income exemption. The second-tier pension, compulsory for employees, is earnings-related and currently pays a married couple, the husband of which has had average earnings for forty years, some $2 200 a month (perhaps 1 800 PPP dollars). There is an element of redistribution in the operation of this pension, the dividing line between gainers and losers being currently, according to one calculation, at the monthly salary level of $1 550.[16] A partial opt-out from this tier was introduced in the 1970s – Japan's method of accommodating corporations' desire to use pensions as loyalty motivators – and took the form of a partial 'delegation' of the state earnings-related scheme to firms, allowing them to build top-up schemes with extra (tax-deductible) contributions under quite tight regulatory constraints. There is another system of corporate pensions known as the 'tax-qualified' scheme, under slightly looser regulatory control. Corporate pensions, measured by assets, split 72 : 28 between the two schemes. There are also a number of so-called 'Mutual-Aid' schemes for state and local government employees, a voluntary earnings-related state scheme for the self-employed, and a special mutual fund for employees in small and medium enterprises.

In terms of accumulated assets, the corporate private pension funds amount to some 14 per cent of GDP in 1999, and individuals have another 16 per cent in life insurance funds – a far cry from the figures of close to 100 per cent for both Britain's pension funds and the total assets of insurance companies. At the same time public pension funds, including those for state employees amount to something over 40 per cent of GNP – largely thanks to the fact that the core earnings-related fund – a legacy from those years in the 1960s and 1970s when large cohorts of young people were paying in and few taking out – has built up a buffer 'float' with the equivalent of about 5 years' current benefit payments. (By comparison the US social security fund's float is said to be around 1.1 years' benefits, and Germany's 0.4.)

As for household savings other than in pensions schemes, much of which may nevertheless be savings for old age, the average Japanese household has net savings equivalent to 140 per cent of annual income, of which 45 per cent are bank deposits, nearly 20 per cent life insurance and 11 per cent traded securities, while the state bank, the post-office savings bank, held 40 per cent of the total bank deposits (1999 figures. Japan, Statistics Bureau, Savings Survey).

The 2000 Revisions

Already, in 1981, one of the most trenchant of the Administrative Reform Committee reports, issued under the chairmanship of the austere Doko Toshio, was voicing the view that 'taking individual responsibility' was all-important, that the dreadful state-welfare-dependency of Britons and Swedes should be seen as an awful warning, and that the social security system should concentrate on looking after people who could not help themselves.[17] However, that was then very much a minority view. Starting with the 1985 consolidation of the basic pension and the earnings-related pension into a single system albeit with separate funds, most of the subsequent changes were marginal amendments. It is only in the last five years that 'individual responsibility' and 'safety net' (significantly it is the English word which is imported) have become taken-for-granted slogans, code words for efforts substantially to change the system.

A system which, however, the Ministry of Health and Welfare has made it its mission to defend. It set the parameters of the debate at the end of 1998 with a white paper which set out five alternative scenarios for dealing with demographic change over the next 30 years. The first four were variations on the theme, keep contributions at level x (their present 15 per cent of annual earnings, or 20 per cent, or 25 per cent or 30 per cent) and balance the books by a *y* per cent cut in benefits or a *z* year postponement of the pensionable age. The fifth alternative was the radical one: 'get rid of everything except the equal-for-all basic pension and privatize the rest'. As was doubtless intended the last solution had few supporters.

The final solution – final for this round of discussion – enacted into law in the spring of 2000, was an intermediate, '*cutback ma non troppo*'. The major elements were as follows.

First, there was effectively a cut in the basic flat-rate pension, henceforth to be linked to the cost of living not average earnings, with the proviso that when the gap between the pension thus calculated and the pension as it would have been if linked to earnings reaches 20 per cent, there will be adjustment. It was also accepted in principle that the tax contribution to the pension is to be gradually raised, as public finances permit over the next ten years, from one-third to one-half. This is a concession to those, starting with the government's Social Security Deliberation Commission in 1977, who argue that it should be wholly tax-financed. That argument has become stronger as the number of non-paying delinquents has increased and the efforts to exhort conformity (only five cases have ever been brought to court) have raised administrative costs to 10.5 per cent of contributions, (compared with 0.6 per cent for the employee earnings-related scheme.)[18] Over and above the obvious public finance reason for the reluctance to accept that argument, there is also the 'people shouldn't get something for nothing' argument. In the official propaganda, however, this is put in collectivist rather than individualist terms. There is no pretence that there is a fund into which you pay your money in order to get it back later. The pay-as-you-go nature of the system is acknowledged and treated as a virtue: the contribution is spoken of as a 'remittance' from the earning child generation to the retired parent generation. You earn the right to similar treatment when you are old, by paying up for the old people now.

The changes in the earnings-related tier involved a 5 per cent reduction in the ratio by which new pensions are calculated from the earnings record – to be implemented gradually (the expectation is that it will be over about 12 years) by the percentage at which the rise in nominal earnings exceeds the cost-of-living increase. This is calculated, with the basic pension, to give a 60 per cent replacement rate for a married couple. Second, there is to be a gradual raising of the pensionable age, in stages between 2013 and 2025, from 60 to 65 for men.

It is calculated that whereas, without these amendments, contributions (split 50 : 50 between employer and employee) would have had to rise from 17.35 per cent of monthly earnings to 34.5 per cent (which, in annual terms, since bonuses are not subject to contributions is from 13.6 to 26.7 per cent) this will permit holding them to about 20 per cent annually – and the charge will be spread over bonuses as well as monthly salary.

As many other governments have found, postponing cuts so that those near retirement and thinking seriously about pensions are not much affected, and promising younger generations relief from higher contributions, does effectively dampen opposition to pension trimming. The only organized body of opposition was the Rengo trade union federation which, however, now has few spokesmen in the Diet, and those spokesmen are buried within the Democratic Party whose mainstream is made up of, if anything, even more 'personal responsibility' marketist reformers than the government coalition. Rengo does, however, have representatives on the main Social Security Commission. (These lay *shingikai*, made up of representatives of interest associations plus independents, are appointed 'policy communities' which provide a sounding board for policy initatives, and are still an important part of the constitutional structure.) They did succeed in gaining marginal modifications of the original proposals.

New Departures

The autumn of 1999 and the spring of 2000 saw two other major pieces of social security legislation brought before the Diet. The first was a scheme of compulsory insurance for long-term care, a means, if you like, of pooling on a society-wide basis, the risk we all share of not being able to manage a quick clean death. (To die *pokkuri* is the cheerful Japanese word for it. There are even *pokkuri* shrines where old ladies can go to pray that they should never be reduced to helpless dependence on their daughter-in-law.) As in Germany, and the other northern European countries which have enacted similar schemes, long-term care insurance is evidence of the survival of a sense of social solidarity, and of the legitimacy of the state as an organ for implementing its expression. (The Kobe earthquake and the ad hoc activity of large numbers of spontaneous volunteers did provide the occasion for transplanting to Japan the American advocacy of not-for-profit organizations and the anti-bureaucracy, anti-state 'civil society' philosophy that goes with it, but this seems to be almost tangential to discussions of issues like long-term care.)

The second piece of legislation was one which was to provide the framework for, and to specify the tax exemptions designed to promote, defined contribution pensions, of the kind described earlier.

An essential part of the background to this proposal was the difficulty corporate pension funds had been getting into. A brief historical exegesis may be in order. When modern personnel systems got going in the first half of the century they inherited, (as indeed did Italian firms), a practice of paying workers at the end of their career, a lump-sum 'thank-you' gratuity. With the growth of enterprise unions and the conversion of traditional paternalism to contractual welfare corporatism, these became transformed into gratuities paid as of right according to previous salaries and years of service. In reasonably prosperous firms in the 1960s, the bonus could amount, after forty years' service, to four or five years' wages, but, even if there had been a developed annuity market, they were rarely sums which would have provided substantial lifetime pensions. As people began to live longer and have fewer children, the state pension scheme, moved in to fill the gap. Corporations, however, still wanted to have schemes which had the additional function of reinforcing loyalty.

Two types of schemes were introduced in 1962–66. The first was integrated into the state earnings-related scheme. Firms could receive 'partial delegation'. That is to say they could keep a part of the contributions paid and add such additional contributions as they were willing to pay, or their union would agree to their workers contributing, to build up a pension fund to enhance the benefits received. The profits of the fund's investment were untaxed (though exempt from the 1988 One Percent Special Corporation Tax only up to a limit of 2.7 times the amount attributable to the 'partial delegation'), but there were prudential restrictions on the classes of investment which could be made, and the fund was required to make a 5.5 per cent rate of return, and to design the relation between contributions and expected benefits accordingly. Since the benefits mostly took the form of lifetime pensions, often with a surviving spouse guarantee, the calculation of the fund's liabilities left considerable scope for obscurity and optimism.

The alternative scheme (the *tekikaku* scheme, usually translated as 'tax-qualified' – meaning tax-exemption qualified) had its legislative foundation only in a set of tax provisions provided for exemptions, and was not subject to the monitoring provided by the 'partial delegation'. Contributions were tax-free. The investment profits of the funds were originally untaxed, but unlike the 'partial delegation' funds, became wholly subject to the 1 per cent Special Corporation Tax – which was widely considered to be unfair discrimination. They were all defined benefit funds. There was no restriction on the form in which benefits were paid, but in practice the dominant form for this type of scheme has been a lump sum, plus pensions paid for ten years only.

For complex reasons the former scheme predominated in the electrical industry, the latter in older industries like steel and in smaller firms.

In the last few years a number of different factors have put these corporate pension plans under quite intense pressure.

1. The recession, zero interest rates, low bond rates, and the fall in land prices, have played havoc with investment returns. The government has responded by relaxing regulations – reducing, then removing, the target interest rate for the 'partial delegation' type funds, removing the restrictions on classes of investment – but that has not solved the fundamental problem. Many corporate plans are clearly underfunded. As the recession has brought bankruptcies, many pensioners have been left with pay-outs of only 20 or 30 per cent of what they had expected. Hitachi, which had for many years been estimating its pension liabilities according to the rigorous Federal Accounting Standard 87 in deference to its quotation on the New York Stock Exchange, decided to cure the underfunding of its own scheme with a large injection of funds in 1997 – equivalent to about 6 per cent of annual revenues, or a tenth of its paid-up capital.
2. The pressures of recession and the vogue for 'restructuring', has brought an increase in the number of mergers. When one firm has a 'partial delegation' plan and the other an 'eligible exemption' plan, their melding can be difficult.
3. Although, with the recession, there has been no great increase in labour mobility, a flexible and active high-turnover labour market is one of the goals of the reformers. This has put the portability of pensions on the agenda.
4. A key tenet of the financial services globalizers is the need for transparency of corporate accounts in order to serve global investors – and particularly, a much discussed question in Germany,[19] for the convenience of investment banks seeking to evaluate a firm for takeover purposes. Currently Japan is in the process of enacting changes in the legal standards for company accounts which will involve compulsory consolidation of subsidiaries' accounts, a large measure of market-valuation for assets, and rigorous criteria for the calculation of pension liabilities. Underfunding is consequently going to become more difficult to conceal.

What seemed like an attractive answer to all these problems was to shift from defined benefit pensions plans to defined contribution plans. Companies would no longer face the prospect of having to make large injections of cash to top up their funds, since the investment risk would be shifted to employees: their benefits would not be guaranteed by the company but depend on the profitability of the type of investment which they individually choose to make. Pension liabilities would disappear and there would be that much less to blur the transparency of company balance sheets. A legislated legal framework could make the same scheme available to self-employed and employees alike. It would also make pension entitlements portable from company to company, and from employment to self-employment, without loss.

Moreover, nothing could be more ideologically attractive to the reformers. It embodied the principle of 'individual responsibility', it would encourage risk-taking and thus help to breed the entrepreneurial culture which could give Japan its own dynamic Silicon Valleys: it would add depth to financial markets. It would also, though this was not an argument often used, bring added business and profits to the people operating in those markets.

What is more, the shift from defined benefit to defined contribution pensions was well under way in the United States, it was one of the secrets of America's economic success, and was therefore a sign of desirable modernity, a fitting reform with which to enter the twenty-first century. It is significant that the proposals were almost universally known as 401k plans – the article in the American tax regulations which governs the US version of the plan. By mid-2000 over twenty books with 401k in the title had been published to explain the arcane mysteries of the American system and the benefits it could bring to Japan. Very few of them pointed out that the American tax exemptions – which could allow up to $25,000 to be invested tax-free into such schemes – were intended to encourage saving in a country which perennially undersaved, and that Japan had the opposite problem of excess savings, and was suffering from low growth rates in large part because its consumers would not spend.

Proposals Whittled Down

The most enthusiastic supporters of the scheme within the bureaucracy were in MITI, which has also been the driving force in measures to promote corporate governance reforms to enhance shareholder sovereignty, unwind cross-shareholdings, and enlarge the scope of venture capital and the stock market. It was hoping that the legislation governing the scheme would provide substantial tax exemptions to get it off the ground and to start a landslide process of transformation of existing defined benefit schemes to a defined contribution basis. The same hope was shared by a group of LDP members of Parliament, of whom the most prominent was Ota Seichi who was also an influential promoter of corporate governance reform. Of the other ministries involved, the Ministry of Health and Welfare had very strong turf-protection reasons for opposing anything that was going to undermine the existing schemes and its own control over their management. Moreover its junior ranks contained fewer of MITI's advocates of dynamic risk-taking, more who were attuned to the security-conscious risk-adversity of the general population. The Ministry of Labour, always ambiguously poised between the labour unions and management, was happy to go along with the reformist rhetoric and had no particular principle to defend. It was the fourth and all-powerful ministry, Finance, which in the end called the shots.

The scheme as it developed took two forms – one primarily for self-employed individuals who could sign up for schemes operated by private financial companies, the other, group schemes for companies which would contract the asset management to the same companies. In either case the pension accounts would be individual. Employees of companies with existing pension schemes could only join a scheme run by their company. Companies which had no scheme could opt for a group one for their employees, but if they chose not to do so, their employees could sign up for an individual pension. Each stakeholder would be given a choice of three investment packages, at least one of which had to be an option which guaranteed no loss of the original capital, such as a bond or bank deposit. The choice could be revised once a year. The crucial question was who should be given tax exemptions and for how large a contribution.

In many respects the final measure fell far short of the expectations of the promoters.

1. The Ministry of Health and Welfare was, in the first instance, insistent that this could only be a 'second pillar' pension, and that not being a 'contribution delinquent' for the basic pension was a precondition for entering the scheme.
2. The tax exemption for the self-employed for whom this was to be their sole 'second pillar' was held down to 86000 yen (about $780) a month.
3. One early point at issue was whether the wives of employees, whose social security is guaranteed by their husband's contributions, (and who already have the privilege of earning a sizeable sum as secondary earners without social insurance or tax contributions) should also be allowed to boost the family post-retirement income with a tax-privileged individual defined contribution (DC) pension. The final answer was no.
4. For the employed, it was assumed that the existing defined benefit schemes, if the company had one, would remain intact, and that any contributions to a defined contribution scheme would be additional. They were therefore set at a maximum of 17000 yen (about $165) a month and were to be wholly paid by the employer. Employees could not make additional contributions and they were not eligible for individual DC schemes.

All this was at the insistence of the Taxation Bureau of the Ministry of Finance, whose dominant concern was to minimize revenue loss, and who countered every citation of the tax-generosity of the American model with the argument that the demand-deficient Japanese economy at the moment had need of incentives to dissave not to save. The anticipated final bill – the revenue cost of introducing the scheme under plausible estimates of take-up – was 14 billion yen (about \$127 million) – about half of the value of new tax concessions on home loans designed to pep up the housing market.

But according to a MITI official who was of the opinion that the pension system needed drastic reform because the social safety net had been set too high, there was also, in the move to cut back the scope of the scheme, a strong element of 'bashing anything that favoured the rich' (*kanemochi yuugu no bashing*).

The bill was finally introduced into the Diet in the spring of 2000, but priority was given to the bill reforming the public pension system and it did not get enacted. Given the choice of abandoning the bill or passing it over to the next session, the LDP managers decided to abandon it in order that it should not become an issue (i.e., a liability, an unpopular issue) in the June elections. It was reintroduced during the emergency session of the autumn and finally enacted in the spring ordinary session, 2001.

After all the brave talk of a new pensions era, it has been somewhat of a let-down for the bill's promoters. The American Chamber of Commerce, Japan has sent the government strongly-worded memoranda urging both early enactment and enlargement of scope. And one of the bill's sponsors in the LDP (a member of a group of 'second-generation' MPs who have inherited their fathers' seats and picked up an American business school training on the way) used a speech at the Japan Society New York to reassure his listeners that Japan would 'keep its promises' and make sure the law was enacted. Meanwhile corporations have gone distinctly cool on the idea of DC schemes, given the severe limitations of the present measure. (While the urgency of doing something about their pension fund was somewhat blunted by their fiscal 1999 experience of getting a 13 per cent return on assets – thanks to the vagaries of the stock market, which have subsequently given them negative returns again.)

This has also blunted the enthusiasm with which DC plans are being prepared. Two major Japanese groups are at work, but they are said to be far from ready. Only Fidelity, which is a major operator of such schemes in the United States, was ready to go by autumn 1999. It is not unreasonable to suppose that its less well prepared Japanese rivals were not unhappy with the delay in enacting the bill.

The State-Market Balance

So, for the moment, the redistribution of labour income through payroll and other taxes and PAYG pensions seems likely to continue to be the mainstream. Japanese savings are going to remain more modest in proportions and to find their way into the global economy through bank lending, rather than through asset managers operating in secondary markets all over the globe. The number of voters with a direct interest in global financial markets – who might have a strong personal interest in stopping any move towards a national opt-out – is thereby limited.

As far as pensions go, the state-market balance has not tipped decisively in favour of the market and there are no immediate signs that it will soon do so. In this racially and culturally homogeneous society whose members still have a sense of being, collectively, somewhat outside the 'Western' (i.e. Mediterranean-based) culture, there is still enough of a sense of social solidarity to support the collective pooling of risks, and the redistribution of income which it entails. This is evidenced in the new long-term care scheme and also in the way, already mentioned, in which the Japanese pay-as-you-go pension system is explicitly described in the Ministry of Health and Welfare's cartoon pamphlets as a form of remittance from the working child generation to the retired parent generation. In a more individualistic society like Britain, by contrast, the pension system is spoken of as if it were a funded scheme; you pay your contributions now in order to get your money back when you grow old. The Japanese view implies that you trust the government of future generations to do unto you as you do unto the old people now. The British view is that you only trust in the impersonal mechanisms which guarantee you your rights.

THE LONG RUN PROSPECT

So there are no immediate signs of a substantial tipping of the state-market balance, but over the longer term, one cannot be sure. The long-term hopes, or the strategy, of the financial services industry is well set out in a survey of the Japanese economy by the Fuji Securities Research Centre. Commenting on the prospective introduction of the DC pension plan, it acknowledged that it was of limited scope, but it could have a significant impact

> on the future evolution of public pensions. The forthcoming amendment of the system was preceded by a MHW paper which spelt out five alternatives, one of which – one which attracted a great deal of attention – was transformation into a privatized, fully funded system. There was a strong current of opinion that if this were to happen it should be through the introduction of a defined contribution system. This option has not been taken at the moment, but there is a strong body of academic opinion in its favour, and it seems certain to reappear on the reform agenda. There are some, indeed, who advocate, on the Chilean model, the extension of the defined contribution principle even to the basic pension. If the present introduction of the principle goes smoothly, one can anticipate that the, at

present deeply-rooted, opposition to such a development on the part of workers, etc. will gradually weaken.

The second significance of a DC system is the penetration of the principle of individual responsibility for the choice of financial products. In America it is said that the education of workers in such matters after the introduction of the 401k pensions system has had precisely that effect.[20]

In forecasting the future, one can assume that old people have, as voters, a strong interest in maintaining, and even enhancing the generosity of, a state pension system with defined benefits, and as their number increases, governments should become more sympathetic to their views. If, on the other hand, an increasing proportion of the younger have their future assured by individual market-dependent, not state-dependent pensions, their unhappiness with paying contributions to state schemes will increase. And they are likely to be the more educated, the more articulate, part of the electorate with the highest incomes, the ones likely to be on the losing end of any intragenerational transfers the state scheme entails. Add to this the persuasive clout of the ever more powerful financial services industry which recruits an ever larger segment of the nation's best brains, and whose lobbying pressure is exerted through personal social ties with individual politicians and not just by the representations of their formal associations. It was a former Japanese Vice-minister of Finance who wrote in 1991: 'the worldwide prevalence of greed among players of the money game poses a serious threat to the healthy development of manufacturing. Promising engineering graduates are lured into financial services while manufacturing firms are more excited about playing money games than creating something tangible'.[21]

An advertising page in the main financial newspaper designed to promote defined contribution pensions schemes (sponsors unnamed) contained an interview with Professor Takenaka from Keio University.[22] His main theme was risk and return. Hitherto the Japanese had been content to put their savings into fixed interest bank deposits or land. The one was low risk low return, the other, because land prices seemed inexorably destined to go on for ever rising, was no risk and super-high returns. Either way they didn't think about risk. But he sees no reason for thinking that the Japanese people are somehow inherently risk-averse. Look at the popularity of horse-racing. What is needed is a process of education. It might not be a bad idea to teach children about stocks and shares in primary school, to implant the idea that taking aboard greater risk can lead to higher returns. The defined contribution pension scheme will help, as it has in America and in Sweden, to create a mechanism for healthy savings to be channelled into risk money.

Notably the words 'speculative' and 'speculation' appeared nowhere in the article, and his reference to the popularity of horse-racing avoided use of the word 'gambling'. (These are still not very nice words in Japan. The lottery is very much a lower-class thing and there seems to be no word equivalent to the English 'flutter' meaning gambling as the occasional harmless entertainment.)

The friend who sent me the cutting is no stranger to financial markets. He was formerly finance director of a Japanese firm which had the distinction of topping the Return on Equity rankings in the mid-1990s, largely because he had resisted the temptation to rake in cheap new equity during the earlier bubble so that his equity base was small. He is anything but enthused by the golden future sketched by Professor Takenaka. 'Do you think that the combat troops of the Japanese corporation, the men who are now so preoccupied with keeping their jobs in these days of universal restructuring that they even neglect their children's education, are going to give their full attention to the management of their assets? Like bringing up the children, it will all be left to their wives, and we'll be lucky if we don't produce a generation of neurotic women.'

My friend is in his late sixties. Professor Takenaka is in his forties. Among the gung-ho young salary-men in their twenties who can soon look forward to being able to buy mutual funds on their internet mobile phones or from their local all-night convenience store, it would doubtless be hard to find anyone who shares my friend's antipathetic doubts about Professor Takenaka's scenario.

CONCLUSION

There can be no doubt about the trend in Japan – towards a long-term gradual shift from collective arrangements to individual arrangements, more people dependent for their income in old age on investments in financial markets, more financial and political power to those who offer to manage their assets for them. The one scenario which might see a reversal of that trend is: such a rapid and universal shift throughout the OECD world from pay-as-you-go to funded pensions, that the savings glut and a secular fall in interest rates becomes obvious enough to change the global conventional wisdom.

But as long as the general belief that the long-term interest rates and risk premia of the next forty years can be extrapolated from the last forty survives such episodes of 'wealth-destruction' as we are experiencing in 2001, the existing trend seems inexorable. A recent memorandum of the American Chamber of Commerce Japan[23] illustrates that inexorability in detailing one mechanism reinforcing those trends – the slow but steady advance of the professional investment advisor, exponent of financial expertise operating to purely financial maximands, replacing generalist bureaucrats with more broadly defined welfare concerns. The legal recognition of licensed investment advisors in Japan and definition of their qualifications came in a law of 1986. Employee pensions funds were authorized to use them in 1990. In 1995 a change in regulations allowed their appointment to oversee certain public pension funds, both those of the civil service itself and the fund of the main social security pension system. At present however, the post office bank and insurance funds are restricted to using trust banks. This is quite wrong, says the ACCJ, because, 'in any industry, consumers, institutional or retail, deserve the opportunity to choose the best provider for different services.' And they point out that if they were allowed to use 'global custodians' Japanese institutional investors would be able to get the best deal for their money anywhere in the world. The truly global custodians, of course, are predominantly American.

Similar stories could be repeated in Germany or in Italy. And with every advance in the size and depth of international capital markets and the global firms which manage them – and the number of people in every country who have a stake in them – the possibility of 'national opt-outs' is diminished. They might be tried said Susan Strange if the economic pain of a systemic crash is great enough. Given the nature of these long-run trends one needs to add; 'and comes soon enough'.

JANUARY 2002 UPDATE

Since this was written (a) the apparent pick-up in the Japanese economy has been nipped in the bud by the shrinkage of the American and European economies; (b) a succession of colourless and ineffective prime ministers has been followed by a new and highly popular one, Koizumi, full of zeal for 'reform' though in ways as yet unspecified. (c) the Defined Contributions Pensions Bill discussed above was passed into law as programmed before the arrival of the new prime minister but launched with enthusiasm by him; (d) the Professor Takenaka whose essay on the virtues of high-risk/high return investments is quoted at the end of the chapter has become Minister of Economic Affairs in Koizumi's cabinet, and is a key figure in drawing up his reform plans – making Japan a true market economy; (e) one of those reforms has been to surrender the post office bank and insurance funds mentioned in the penultimate paragraph to the ministrations of 'truly global investors' as demanded by the American Chamber of Commerce; (f) otherwise the efforts at supply side reforms have consisted primarily of (1) privatization of a number of public corporations – a popular piece of bureaucrat-bashing since they were generally headed by ex-bureaucrats, and (2) pressure on the banks to clear up bad debts; (g) which, producing more bankruptcies (14 listed companies in 2002 with total debts of over $20 billion) and more unemployment has done nothing about the real demand deficiency problem except to exacerbate it. Meanwhile, loose talk, but no specific action, about 'reforming pensions' serves to keep savings too high (especially among the older affluent income earners), while zero nominal interest rates, negative returns on pension funds, and new accounting rules force corporations into excess savings to top up pension funds, thus adding to deflationary pressures and bringing the whole funded pension system – not to mention the whole banking system – into crisis. Mr. Koizumi's place in history as Japan's President Hoover seems assured. It is less clear who will be its FDR.

NOTES

1. Stephen Kobrin (1998), 'MAI and the clash of globalizations', Foreign Policy, 112, (Fall).
2. Philip Augar, *The Death of Gentlemanly Capitalism*, London, Penguin Books, 2000, 307–8.
3. Ibid. p.74.
4. Takayama Noriyuki, *Nenkin no kyooshitsu [Pensions classroom]*, Tokyo, PPH Shuppan, 2000.
5. Luis Cubeddu, 'Intragenerational redistribution in unfunded pension systems', *IMF Staff Papers*, 47, i, 2000, p.102.
6. OECD, 'The macroeconomics of ageing, pensions and savings: A survey', Working Paper AWP 1.1. 1998.
7. Merrill Lynch, Global Securities Research and Economics Group, *Progress Report: European Pension Reforms, Pension Barometer for Europe*, 17 Jan 2001. Of the nine indicators used for the barometer, seven are various ways of measuring public expenditure reduction now and projected. The eighth is the size of pension fund assets, the ninth per capita income of the pensioner population, with no measure of the distribution thereof.
8. Gordon L. Clark, 'European pensions and global finance: continuity or convergence?', School of Geography and Environment, Oxford, mimeo.
9. 'America's economy: What a peculiar cycle', *The Economist*. 10 March 2000, p.73
10. All the following calculations are based on Office of National Statistics, *Family Spending 1998–99*, Table 8.1.
11. Department of Social Security, Dataset ST30526.
12. As the OECD study quoted earlier acknowledges. See para 59.
13. Merrill Lynch, Global Securities Research and Economics Group, *Demographics and the funded pensions system*, 30 October 2000.
14. Richard Cardarelli, James Sefton and Laurence J. Kotlikoff, 'Generational accounting in the UK' *Economic Journal*, November 2000, p.548.
15. Noriyoshi Oguchi and Tatsuo Hatta, 'Switching the Japanese social security system from pay as you go to actuarially fair: A simulation analysis', mimeo, 2001.
16. Oguchi and Hatta, op. cit. The exchange rate used in this paragraph is $1 = ¥110
17. Martin Collick, 'Social policy: pressures and responses' in J.A. Stockwin et al. (eds), *Dynamic and Immobilist Politics in Japan*, Honolulu, University of Hawaii Press, 1988.
18. Takayama, op.cit., p.100.
19. Gordon Clark, Daniel Mansfield and Adam Tickell, 'Accounting standards and German Supplementary Pensions: The emerging framework underpinning global finance', School of Geography and the Environment, Oxford, mimeo.
20. Fuji Sogo Kenkyujo, *2000nen Nihon Keizai no shinro [The way ahead for the Japanese economy in the year 2000]* Tokyo, Chuo Koronsha, p.177.

21. Toyo Gyohten, 'Global financial markets: The past, the future and public policy questions' in F.R. Edwards and H.T. Patrick (eds), *Regulating International Financial Markets: Issues and Policies,* Norwell, MA, Kluwer, 1991, p.18.
22. 'Yutaka na rogo wo jibun de tsukuru' ['Making your own affluent old age'] and 'Risuku to ritaan no kankei, kichin to haaku suru koto ga juyo' ['The important thing: getting a good grasp on the relation of risk and return'] *Nihon Keizai Shimbun,* 26 November 1999, second section.
23. ACCJ, ACCJ Viewpoint, Kampo and Yucho Use of Investment Advisors, 2000.

6. Private Power and Public Authority

Louis W. Pauly

In her pioneering work in the study of international political economy, Susan Strange always placed 'the human condition' at the centre (Palan 1999). One aspect of that condition eventually came to the forefront of her research: the transformation of national political authority as actual structures of power and influence were spilling over territorial boundaries, and increasingly even rendering those boundaries meaningless.[1] In a volume touching on various aspects of that transformation, especially as it appears to be suggested by contemporary developments in international capital markets, it is worth reflecting more deeply on the conceptual and practical relationship between authority and power. Strange herself spent much of her scholarly career probing this very relationship, which lay at the core of the human political condition. Following her example, this chapter probes the relationship, mainly in the context of evident changes in the world of finance, and suggests new directions for future research.

AUTHORITY, POWER, AND INTERNATIONAL FINANCE

Exploring the evolution, trajectory, and meaning of authority in the financial arena is, in truth, intellectually stimulating only to human beings living today in localities conventionally classed as advanced industrial democracies, because only therein lies potential tractability. Much of the rest of humanity would find the exercise quite useless. In the face of globalizing finance, in the halls of Susan Strange's famous 'casino', they are like an unarmed civilian confronting a soldier with a loaded machine gun. They may hope that the gun is wielded wisely and in their own long-run interest. But their ability to ensure such wisdom, or even to encourage it, is limited. They confront, in short, what Bachrach and Baratz described in a famous essay as the 'first face' of power; asymmetries in capabilities and influence are such that the interests of the strong can simply be imposed upon the weak (Bachrach and Baratz 1962).[2] In the case of very weak countries, this is the end of a not very unusual chapter in world history.

Among the privileged few, however, a belief is still commonly shared. It is the belief that the wielding of all instruments of coercion, from military to financial, can and should be subject to a certain degree of control by legitimate and accountable political authorities. Indeed, we citizens of advanced industrial democracies commonly consider the measurement of just such degrees of control to be the measurement of a critically important aspect of the quality of the human condition. Even for those who are sceptical about the degree of that quality in the context of globalizing finance, the underlying distinction between ultimate coercive power and power limited by the necessity to take into account the anticipated reactions of its targets remains important. This, Bachrach and Baratz called the 'second face' of power. At its most sophisticated level, as students of Antonio Gramsci most prominently explain, an ideological mask can render even that necessity invisible as the interests of the weak and the interests of the strong are seamlessly woven together (Gill 1993). With or without the mask, a social relationship resting on such mutual perceptions of gain and mutual aversions to loss makes tangible a traditional conception of political authority. Underpinning the idea of authority is the concept of legitimacy. In terms most often associated with the work of the great German social theorist, Max Weber, a sense of legitimacy is commonly understood to exist when convergent perceptions of entitlement to command and obligation to comply exist between the wielder of power and those subject to that power. Might makes right is the aphorism of coercive power, used or lost. Legitimate rule, conversely, assumes that right makes might more enduring. The distinction is key to understanding the social and political implications of contemporary developments in international financial markets.

Economic historians still argue about the extent and the results of the set of national economic policies widely implemented in the 1930s, policies often branded with the modifier 'beggar-thy-neighbour'. For the American, British, and Canadian designers of the post-World War II international monetary system, perceptions that the modifier was an accurate description of what had actually happened dominated. The 'Keynesian' revolution ushered in a new experiment in fusing power to legitimate social purpose, one which John Ruggie encapsulated in the phrase 'embedded liberalism' (Ruggie 1982). Interdependent, cooperative but still *national* capitalist democracies would balance the search for economic prosperity through international exchange with the maintenance of full political integrity. Internally, they would each in their own ways define and advance the cause of social justice; they would seriously strive to expand opportunities not just for the rich, as had been the case in the first era of global capitalism in the years before World War I, but for the masses. In this new normative environment, Keynesians dreamed that international monetary control could be maintained by interdependent political authorities willing to subordinate a natural and historically justified sense of distrust to a common cause (Helleiner 1994). Spreading international economic prosperity would underpin national security and usher 'the second great age of global capitalism' (Gilpin 2000, Ch. 2).

As a profound Keynesian, but one who never lost a clear-eyed sense of scepticism, and one who always understood the intimate linkage between the American-led nuclear security structure and the new international economy, Strange was among the first analytically to dissect the machinery of governance placed at the centre of the postwar experiment (Kirshner 2000, 408). By the early 1970s, she had witnessed that machinery becoming overwhelmed by resurgent market forces. Monetary matters became the focal point for sustained attention early on in her career as a scholar. In particular, she observed and described the International Monetary Fund, the keeper of the Keynesian dream, gradually being sidelined by burgeoning financial markets as well as by narrowly self-regarding American policy preferences. She would later see the same pattern emerging in many other arenas.

From her first major book to her last, Strange probed the fundamental implications of global finance for modern social democracy, imperfect as it was but whose gains were achieved at such horrendous cost in blood and treasure during her lifetime. She was way ahead of her time in asking a question that would become urgent as the constituent elements of a truly global economy began to come together in the latter decades of the twentieth century. What did the rise of a new global elite, increasingly freed from the obligations of local civil societies, mean for a hard-won democratic understanding of the nature of political authority, an understanding that now rested on a basic sense of social solidarity and an expectation of both individual and collective autonomy? Even to ask the question was to beg the sceptical answer. Who would rule, how would they rule, and in whose interest would they rule? Strange did not shy away from demanding answers from members of the new global elite themselves.

GLOBAL MONEY, LOCAL AUTHORITY

The central question becomes clearer after a few distinctions are drawn. Benjamin J. Cohen proposes a key one in *The Geography of Money* (1998). Therein he separates for analytical purposes the supply side of money from the demand side. On the demand side, like Strange in *Mad Money*, he sees a profound contemporary blurring of the nature of monetary power within many states and across the international system as a whole. On the supply side, however, and like Strange in her early work on the international monetary system, he depicts a more traditional movement from multipolar to unitary and again to multipolar orders – all based upon a traditional territorial notion of public political authority (Strange 1976). Cohen nevertheless goes on to conclude as follows:

> Once we acknowledge the growth of cross-border competition, the state-centric model looks increasingly inadequate, if not wholly misleading. The more widely circulated currencies come to be used across, not just within, political frontiers, the more pivotal becomes the independent role of market forces in global monetary governance. Market agents too exercise power, and they increasingly rival governments as direct determinants of currency outcomes. The strategic interaction between public and private sectors, not between states alone, becomes the primary focus of authority in monetary affairs. (Cohen 1998, 167– 68)

I believe what Cohen means here is that in 'normal' times – periods of relative social and political stability, when war is not underway or imminent, when an economic depression is not occurring, when financial markets are functioning as well as can be expected – a blurring of the locus of ultimate political authority can occur. In this regard, he shares the well-known position Strange took in her final days, and the argument continues concerning the uniqueness and importance of contemporary episodes of monetary border-blurring. In practical terms, however, and in a way that neither Strange nor he fully set out, Cohen's analysis also implies that the peculiar constitution of political authority as developed most fully in the now-dominant United States might be extending itself around the world through the expansion of global finance. In such a system of governance, formal power is divided, decision-making is deliberately complicated, distributive questions are addressed as often as possible through blame-diffusing private markets, and an underlying sense of legitimacy derives both from a flawed but functioning representative democracy and from an ideology evoked by the phrase 'manifest destiny'.[3]

A clearer distinction needs to be made here between the language of power and the language of authority. As Strange reminded us, both in *Casino Capitalism* and in *Mad Money*, episodes of crisis might tell us more about the nature of political authority in a given instance than do episodes in calmer times. Despite the obfuscation of accountability always implied in regimes – like the political economy in place within the United States – often aiming to advance public policy agendas through the indirect means of private but orderly markets, actual crises in the waning years of the twentieth century continued to suggest that national governments would be blamed for financial catastrophes in the new world of globalizing finance. At least some of them, moreover, retained the full authority necessary to respond.

It is true that such statements as 'governments can opt out of global capital markets' are close to vacuous when no crisis looms. The economic and political costs of doing so, as Cohen points out, would be astronomically high. Imagine, for example, what kind of political calculus would be needed today to encourage, say, Canada to revert to a regime of extensive exchange controls. But such a calculus is only implausible to imagine, not impossible. States under unusual stress defy conventional economic wisdom all the time, unless, of course, they can't. As Ron Dore puts it in his chapter in this book, when international capital markets expand and deepen 'the possibility of national opt-outs' diminishes, certainly in practice if not in theory. But in a collective sense, in neither global nor regional domains have we yet experienced circumstances where that diminishment has reached the vanishing point.

Recall once again the Weberian idea of legitimacy, a shared belief grounding an intimate relationship between leaders and followers and thereby constituting authority. By an analogous standard, and linguistic custom, a mother has authority over her child; its existence can be demonstrated when, say, even the hint of a disappointed frown, much less than the back of a hand, is enough to reverse inappropriate behaviour. The obligation to obey is hard-wired into the child's world-view. Over time, the rules of the game, a framework of regularity and, ultimately, a sense of trust and expectation, become so deeply entrenched that they enter the realm of the unconscious. The parallels between such a simple example of what might be termed 'private authority' and more general cases of public authority are easy to draw but complicated to spell out. Strange herself had a deep understanding of the complex relationship between political legitimacy and coercive power in the constitution of public authority, a relationship that must form the foundation for any progressive as well as hard-headed view of the present moment of global transformation.

In today's capital markets, at least, the emergence of what can look like the private usurpation of public authority may well be a contingent and fleeting phenomenon. The volatility and fragility of those markets, which worried Strange deeply, could themselves be viewed as reflective of the quality of public authorities lying beneath their surface and of the changing nature of relationships among those authorities.[4] As the world witnessed in the late 1990s – from the IMF-led operation to keep Russia and South Korea solvent to the privately financed but publicly supervised bailout of the US-based Long Term Capital Management hedge fund in September 1998, at moments of supreme crisis in those markets, public authority itself could still be reasserted. The private authority some see evolving as market deepening occurs, in the crunch proves ephemeral.

Yes, one can hear the voice of Susan Strange responding, but for how long? Ron Dore's conclusion echoes her *cri de coeur* with good reason. Will we not soon reach the point where private authority becomes so strong that such responses become improbable? Worse, are we not soon at the point where no one is truly accountable or responsible for the health and safety of the world's financial markets?

One test of the underlying presence of legitimate public authority in those markets might be conceived as follows. When decisions are taken through them to privatize gains and socialize losses, are those decisions acquiesced in by the relevant citizenry in whose name they occur, or do they become rallying points for revolt? It could be that when such acquiescence occurs, it depends upon the perception on the part of citizens that though a loser today, they or their children might be winners tomorrow. Just such a perception seems to justify decisions most obviously and consistently taken in American national markets whenever systemic catastrophe has loomed ever since 1929. When the crisis point arrives in ever more open, ever more 'deregulated' markets, the state steps back in. The face of that state most often resembles the Federal Reserve, but no one doubts that the US Treasury and the US Congress reside in the background.

The really interesting questions in this regard are the ones that Strange was just beginning explicitly to ask. A now-commonplace metaphor became in her hands an urgent new challenge. What if the main international financial markets are ever-closer tables in a true casino, where at least the possibility of iterated, non-zero-sum games is replaced by the certainty that each game is rigged and, in the long-run, that only the house can win? And what if the owners of the house, moreover, are becoming a new class of plutocrats – more numerous than their predecessors in the gilded age but behaviourally not dissimilar, a new class essentially accountable to no one but itself, and with technocrats at various levels of governance essentially responsible to it?

We may not be quite there yet, and booming markets have a tendency to shroud such questions, and even to push them off the public agenda. But busting markets may be counted upon to bring them back. Observing the wax and wane of markets all her life, it became clear to Strange that advanced industrial states and their citizens were engaged late in the twentieth century in a very real struggle over the restructuring of that house and, yes, whether they used the term or not, over the re-regulation of the casino. For the theorists amongst us, the parallel inquiry revolves around how we might understand and relate the ideological and practical factors conditioning that restructuring, a process implicating much more than financial markets and a process evoked by the term globalization. In other words, we are asking how political authority is actually being reconstituted today. Underneath such an enquiry, and David Calleo's chapter in this volume provides a good example, we are reflecting on how should it be reconstituted, precisely in order to avoid the realization of Strange's nightmare scenario. The roots of resistance to anti-democratic and unjust movements in this regard are beginning to be probed not just in the transnational sphere, but also and perhaps more importantly in the local.

At the end of her life, Strange put the central matter succinctly:

> We are talking about relative values and social preferences – the preference, for example, for more equity and more stability [. . .] for the quality of economic growth rather than its quantity [. . .]. That is what debates in international political economy and in theoretical economics ultimately boil down to. [But] political choices are formed by people's experience. Our problem in the next century is that the traditional authority of the nation state is not up to the job of managing mad international money, yet its leaders are instinctively reluctant to entrust that job to unelected, unaccountable (and often arrogant and myopic) bureaucrats. We have to invent a new kind of polity but we cannot yet imagine how it might work. (Strange 1998, 190)

THE RECONSTITUTION OF POLITICAL AUTHORITY?

From Canada to Europe to East Asia in the 1990s, the contours of power in monetary affairs seemed to shift dramatically. In the former case, the Board of Governors of the Federal Reserve System seemed to loom ever larger in a monetary policy that was only at the margins made-at-home. In Europe, an experiment in pooling monetary sovereignty was launched. In East Asia, as financial crisis swept through the region in the late 1990s, the assertion of the Malaysian prime minister that international financiers were deliberately destabilizing the national economy resonated around the world and set alarm bells ringing from Wall Street to the City of London. But what did such cases imply for the fundamental transformation of political authority? In this regard, the appropriate litmus test cannot be designed on the basis of some unrealistic notion of Westphalian sovereignty, which was in any event historically always much more contested than is often assumed (Krasner 1999). Once again, Dore is absolutely right to call attention in his chapter to the polemical morass created by the disembodied concept of national 'opt-outs' in the complex system of relationships constituting modern capitalism. As Dore and Strange both point out repeatedly in their work, the relative costs of staying in would have to become very high indeed (and the relative benefits correspondingly low) for states in the system actually to consider opting out. But the test of when economic interdependence reaches the point where something fundamental has changed in the very constitution of political authority in those states is much more prosaic.

When Canada and the United States agree that the Bank of Canada will become another regional bank within the Federal Reserve System, or when Canada unilaterally decides to adopt the US dollar as its domestic currency, then something fundamental will have occurred in the nature of political authority within its territory.[5]   When a Latin American country has done something very close to this, say, through a rigid currency board arrangement based on US dollars, and when its policymakers have convinced international financiers and powerful domestic interests that they cannot reverse such a course even if they and their constituents demand it, then something fundamental will have occurred in the nature of political authority there.[6] When European monetary union forces member states to coordinate their fiscal policies more deeply, something fundamental will be occurring in the location and quite probably in the nature of political authority among them.

Such developments may be imagined, and the latter even seems well underway.   But short of such dramatic changes, most of the world's population remains in an environment of intensifying interdependence, an environment where those 'in authority' find their policy options ever more severely constrained by a changing distribution of power among themselves. They exist, in short, at the intersection of the private and the public spheres as they themselves have constructed them.

Let me emphasize once more that this ancient distinction between authority and power is hardly a matter of interest only to pedants. Indeed, the desire to avoid fundamental changes in the nature of political authority in the new world of international capital mobility may be understood to provide the driving force behind the round after round of multilateral efforts to clarify, strengthen, and rationalize the mandates of international financial institutions. The same dynamic reinforces internal pressures within many states to move toward 'independent' central banks so as to provide more durable political buffers for markets and governments. In the best case, such state-created technocratic agencies at either international or national levels promise to promote adequate standards of financial regulation and supervision around the world, design functional programmes for crisis avoidance and crisis management, and provide workable mechanisms – 'architecture' in the now-popular parlance – for governments credibly to collaborate with one another for mutual benefit. In the worst case, such agencies can take on the role of scapegoats, thus serving to limit the political fallout from local crises that would inevitably follow any systemic financial catastrophe.   What technocratic agencies have difficulty addressing, however, are basic questions of social justice. Not only are standards across diverse societies themselves still diverse, but those agencies are expected to help manage a system where the mobility of capital is not matched by the mobility of people.

Social justice, political legitimacy, and effective authority are today
inextricably linked concepts. At the systemic level, they become so abstract
as to be meaningless. It was not always this way, and it may not be at some
time in the future. But today they infuse actual institutions and practice
almost exclusively at the local but sometimes at the regional levels. In the
current international monetary and financial system, the distance between
them and empirical evidence reflects the fact that the governments of states
cannot now shift ultimate political authority to the level of governance
suggested by the term global finance. And even if they wanted to, surely the
vast majority of their citizens would object. Only in Europe, within the
restricted context of a regional economic experiment still shaped by the
legacy of the most catastrophic war in world history, was a difficult-to-
reverse shift in political authority beyond the national level in sight. And
even there, where so much movement has recently occurred, the path to the
fundamental reconstruction and relocation of authority remained a winding
one.[7]

Elsewhere in the industrial world, the citizens of still-national states seek
the benefits of international capital mobility without paying the ultimate
political costs implied by true integration. 'Global markets' are themselves
political projects. Stabilizing those markets is an unavoidable aspect of that
experiment, and it involves two dimensions: managing systemic risk and
ensuring that modicum of symmetry in adjustment burdens required to
sustain the logic of interdependence, or at least to keep the coercive face of
modern capitalism as veiled as possible.

Sometimes the power to stabilize markets may be seized by or delegated to
the private sector. Self-regulatory organizations, as oxymoronic as the term
sounds, are nothing new in a capitalist system, especially when Anglo-Saxon
or American liberalism provides the framework for policy action or inaction.
When such efforts accomplish their goals, the dog does not bark, catastrophes
are avoided. But when such efforts fail, or threaten to fail, one of two things
seem to happen, even in England and America. Agents of legitimate public
authority take back regulatory power, or markets collapse. It is at least
arguable therefore that the emergence of what can look like the private
usurpation of public authority is a contingent and fleeting phenomenon. Such
a contention needs to be fleshed out by pushing toward more comprehensive
as well as more rigorous theory, and by explicating that theory against the
backdrop of an explicitly justified interpretation of history.

POWER POLITICS, NETWORKS OF INTERDEPENDENCE, AND THE NEW WORLD OF MONEY

At the analytical heart of a new project to theorize the changing politics of money is a straightforward puzzle that immediately arises if one cannot accept the premise that politics can ever really be assumed away. How can the liberal internationalist vision at the core of the twentieth-century movement toward deepening economic interdependence and integration be squared with the continuing reality of dispersed and asymmetrical political power? And how is true authority to rule reshaped at the new intersection between international finance and international politics? Globalization and power politics fit as uneasily together now as they did one hundred years ago, when a liberal world economy first became a focal point for the fundamental re-ordering of humanity.

One line of answers begins with the assertion that real power is not really dispersed: we live in a quasi-imperial political structure centred on the United States.[8] Calleo's chapter herein provides a stimulating example. My own earlier exploration of the meaning and scope of IMF operations in the advanced industrial world, however, leads me to doubt this answer, or at least to insist on a nuanced view of the American capacity actually to play the imperial role (Pauly 1997). Later work on cultures of corporate control in Germany and Japan reinforce doubts about the true extent, durability, and effectiveness of the coercive power of the United States. To be sure, plenty of what Joseph Nye calls 'soft power' emanates from an American base. But it remains quite easy for the nimble, the determined, and the smart to manipulate the relatively open system through which that power filters. It also remains quite debatable whether such power as the United States obviously possesses is always wielded for wholly constructive purposes. With deference not always readily forthcoming in its external realm, the nature of its hegemony remains problematic. The self-serving rhetoric of peripatetic investment bankers and the awesome images of Stealth bombers acting in the name of the 'international community' need to be assessed as sceptically as Calleo implies. Better to start with a sense of a reality more complex, contingent, and ambiguous.

A second common approach to the global economy/local politics dialectic begins with the assumption that more or less efficient and automatic market mechanisms now exist to encourage more or less consistent movement toward cooperative international outcomes. From the start, however, empirical support is weak. Just a short time ago, in the midst of the East Asian financial crisis, even stalwart proponents of the liberal internationalist project publicly expressed their fears that a new Great Depression loomed. But the deeper problem with this approach lies in its logical circularity. More or less well-functioning markets spreading prosperity and encouraging long-term system-stabilizing adjustments – cooperative outcomes in the face of contrary economic and political phenomena – are ultimately the thing-to-be-explained by any theory worthy of the name. They cannot do the explaining too.

An alternative approach could begin with the following line of argument. Increasingly global markets are the fruit of intensifying interaction among still-mainly-national political systems. In such a context, and in the contemporary period, conflicting visions of the requirements of political legitimacy become ever more salient and important. That interaction is increasingly buffered mainly by international political organizations but now also by an emerging array of non-governmental organizations and social movements. At the centre of processes of adaptation in the mandates and capabilities of key international organizations in the economic and financial arena, and also pushing NGOs toward greater visibility, is an ever more obvious struggle between liberal visions of world order based on procedural fairness and enduring alternative visions aiming at distributive justice. Wherever that struggle is joined lies the arena where the seeds of global authority are potentially being sown, either to flourish or to fall by the wayside. The final destiny of any such seeds, however, remains a function mainly of the structures of actual governance within the dominant centres of real political authority within the system.[9]

Such linked propositions may be spun out further to open theoretically-informed research pathways. Domestic politics within still-distinct but more open polities exerts the most determinative influence on the under-structure of an emerging global economy. A hierarchy based sometimes on coercive power but perhaps more often on more subtle forms of influence continues to exist among those polities.[10] The more powerful, in effect, continue their attempts to make the world 'safe' for their own political structures and imperatives, which are themselves deeply rooted but not static. The weaker adapt as much as necessary but as little as possible to achieve their own political objectives, including the retention of the maximum feasible degree of relative autonomy within an integrating system. Sometimes, as perhaps in the Japan explored in Dore's chapter, this may mean going along with the powerful on the surface but resisting under the surface. (Things may indeed be different now, but the question is essentially an empirical one.) In this context, formal multilateral organizations play an ever more, not less, important role. Beyond providing a legal and normative foundation for integration, such a role seems now to include the reshaping of domestic interests in areas close to expanding organizational mandates. Over time, the character, scope, and influence of particular organizations change, even if objective measures of their raw power do not pick this up. The most prominent example in recent years is in the mandate of the International Monetary Fund for 'structural adjustment', which remains unmatched by the financial resources necessary actually to implement its underlying principles (Pauly 1999). To describe such changes as cooperative would be to put an overly benign face on them. In their absence, however, truly global markets would remain only a liberal dream.

A key objective in research along these lines would be to demonstrate how important international organizations focused on cross-border economic and financial integration were actually adapted as debates over justice and fairness played out in crucial domestic arenas. Similarly, at a time when many observers are focused on how non-governmental organizations are influencing the international political agenda and building what they call a global civil society, it would seem timely as well to begin tracing the ways in which NGOs and more or less loosely organized social movements might be finding themselves encouraged to adapt to enduring structures of power.[11] The consistency and coherence of that process across concrete cases will render a general argument emphasizing the hard core of state authority and the contingent nature of global interactions more or less plausible. If less, this would turn analysis away from political contingency toward broader determinants of a global economy (again, say, back to the effective directives of a hegemonic state, the force of overwhelming technological imperatives, or the narrow and convergent interests of a specific transnational elite). If more, various theoretical and policy implications may be expected to follow.

Such an argument, indeed, would lead us back to the kind of research Susan Strange undertook in the earliest stage of her academic career. Her studies of decision-making in the post-war international monetary order as it then existed, and later of the decline of that order, focused her mind on processes of institutional adaptation that could but did not necessarily compromise a moderate Keynesian vision.[12] At least potentially, similar studies today might actually help to open the conceptual space for rebalancing the imperatives of economic efficiency, political autonomy, and social justice.

The search for such openings led Strange back repeatedly to contemplation of the inner workings of the two polities she at once admired and criticized. The American and European experiments in democratic capitalism, she seemed convinced, were the main venues in which new ideas for systemic renewal would be hatched. The next generation of scholars interested in the true foundations of global governance would have to get as deeply immersed in those experiments as she had once become immersed in post-war international monetary institutions.[13]

That, by the end of her life, Strange came close to discounting the possibility of free markets ever being entirely reconciled with democratic political authority reflected an intuition. Despite it, she retained to the last some hope that human ingenuity and wise political leadership could shape a more promising future. This hope, in turn, reflected something deeper in her worldview. The fundamental reconstitution of political authority in our more complex world will not occur because it must, but only because human beings want it to occur. As Strange herself might have put it, humanity is embarked on a journey toward no inevitable destination, save the ultimate one that should be put off for as long as possible.

NOTES

1. This essay grew out of two papers presented at the annual meeting of the International Studies Association, Los Angeles, March 14– 18, 2000. A short extract from one paper was included in the co-authored concluding chapter of Rosenau et al., 2000.
2. For a recent exploration of the distinction, see Pierson, 2000, 259.
3. For a recent survey of the development and expression of the idea, see Stephanson, 1995.
4. These remarks draw on my chapters in Stubbs and Underhill, 2000 and Hall and Biersteker, 2002.
5. For arguments that come close to asserting that just such a re-constitutionalization is now occurring, see Arthurs, 1999.
6. Argentina appeared to have done this in the 1990s, but the limits of its dollarization experiment were laid bare when it defaulted on its debts and devalued its currency in 2001 and early 2002.
7. For a recent treatment of the underlying theoretical and policy issues involved, see Greven and Pauly, 2000.
8. Gilpin comes close to this position, although he occasionally despairs of the US capacity actually to lead such a system.
9. For a suggestive analysis of the rise of international institutions along these lines, see Gruber, 2000.
10. In the monetary arena, see such a theme traced out in Kirshner, 1997.
11. On the new role of NGOs, see O'Brien et al., 2000.
12. See, for example, Strange, 1974.
13. For antecedents that work analytically at both the internal and the external levels in the monetary and financial arenas, see de Cecco, 1976 and 1979.

REFERENCES

Arthurs, H.W. (1999), 'Constitutionalizing Neo-Conservatisim and Regional Economic Integration,' in Thomas J. Courchene (ed.), *Room to Manoeuvre? Globalization and Policy Convergence*, Montreal: McGill-Queen's University Press, pp. 17– 74.
Bachrach, Peter and Morton S. Baratz (1962), 'The Two Faces of Power,' *American Political Science Review*, vol. 56 (December), 947– 52.
Cohen, Benjamin J. (1998), *The Geography of Money*, Ithaca, NY: Cornell University Press.

de Cecco, Marcello (1976), 'International Financial Markets and U.S. Domestic Policy since 1945', *International Affairs*, vol. 52, 381– 99.

de Cecco, Marcello (1979), 'Origins of the Postwar Payments System,' *Cambridge Journal of Economics*, vol. 3, 49– 61.

Gill, Stephen (ed.) 1993, *Gramsci, Historical Materialism, and International Relations*, Cambridge: Cambridge University Press.

Gilpin, Robert (2000), *The Challenge of Global Capitalism*, Princeton, NJ: Princeton University Press.

Greven Michael Th. and Louis W. Pauly (eds) (2000), *Democracy beyond the State? The European Dilemma and the Emerging Global Order*, Lanham, MD/Toronto, ON: Rowman & Littlefield Publishers and University of Toronto Press.

Gruber, Lloyd (2000), *Ruling the World*, Princeton, NJ: Princeton University Press.

Hall, Rodney and Thomas Biersteker (eds) (2002), *The Emergence of Private Authority in Global Governance*, Cambridge: Cambridge University Press.

Helleiner, Eric (1994), *States and the Reemergence of Global Finance*, Ithaca, NY: Cornell University Press.

Kirshner, Jonathan (1997), *Currency and Coercion*, Princeton, NJ: Princeton University Press.

Kirshner, Jonathan (2000), 'The Study of Money', *World Politics*, vol. 52 (April), 407– 36.

Krasner, Stephen (1999), *Sovereignty: Organized Hypocrisy*, Princeton, NJ: Princeton University Press.

O'Brien, Robert et al. (2000), *Contesting Global Governance: Multilateral Economic Institutions and Global Social Movements*, Cambridge: Cambridge University Press.

Palan, Ronen (1999), 'Susan Strange 1923– 1998: a great international relations theorist', *Review of International Political Economy*, vol. 6 (2), 121– 32.

Pauly, Louis W. (1997), *Who Elected the Bankers? Surveillance and Control in the World Economy*, Ithaca, NY: Cornell University Press.

Pauly, Louis W. (1999), 'Good Governance and Bad Policy: The Perils of International Organizational Overextension,' *Review of International Political Economy*, vol. 6 (4), 401– 24.

Pierson, Paul (2000), 'Increasing Returns, Path Dependence, and the Study of Politics', *American Political Science Review*, vol. 94, 2, 251– 67.

Rosenau, James N. et al. (eds.) (2000), *Strange Power*, Brookfield, VT: Ashgate.

Ruggie, John Gerard (1982), 'International Regimes, Transactions, and Change: Embedded Liberalism in the Postwar Economic Order', *International Organization*, vol. 36 (2), 379– 415.

Stephanson, Anders (1995), *Manifest Destiny: American Expansion and the Empire of Right*, New York: Hill and Wang.

Strange, Susan (1974), 'IMF: Monetary Managers', in Robert Cox, Harold Jacobson et al., *The Anatomy of Influence: Decision Making in International Organization*, New Haven, CT: Yale University Press.

Strange, Susan (1976), 'International Monetary Relations', in Andrew Shonfield (ed.), *International Economic Relations in the Western World, 1959–1971*, vol. 2, London: Oxford University Press.

Strange, Susan (1998), *Mad Money*, Ann Arbor, MI: University of Michigan Press.

Stubbs, Richard and Geoffrey Underhill (eds) (2000), *Political Economy and the Changing World Order*, second edn, Oxford/New York: Oxford University Press.

Postscript

Marcello de Cecco

'The metamorphosis of a series of closed, cartelised, nationally controlled and often segmented financial systems into a transnationally desegmented and marketised space characterised by a high degree of capital volatility and mobility is one of the great and unplanned transformations of the twentieth century' (Underhill 1997).

In the introductory chapter to *Mad Money* Susan Strange quotes this sentence of Geoffrey Underhill as capable of aptly summarizing 'the essence of my own views of the international financial scene in the late 1990s'. It is indeed a powerful and concise summary of what went on in the best part of not only the 1990s, as Strange affirms, and not the whole twentieth century, but, in my view, in the whole of the last fifty years.

Both Underhill and Strange, however, subscribe to a typically Anglo-American, Keynesian *weltanschauung*: transformations tend to be unplanned; they are the unforeseen and unintended consequences of initial causes. But Susan Strange was not always consistent in her adherence to this view. Much of what she wrote in her books dealing with the international monetary and financial system in the postwar period is a powerful description of the forces planning the transformations that took place and pointing to the major culprits. And, although in her enumeration of the main actions and omissions which had caused the Casino Capitalism and Mad Money to prevail she mentioned a few European responsibilities, it is clear that she had a main culprit in mind, the United States, seen both as the home of the largest private transnational actors, multinational banks and companies, and of the US Federal institutions, the Presidential administration, Congress, the Courts of Justice. So concentrated and detailed are her accusations that they have elicited the spirited response, among many others, of two eminent contributors to this volume, David Calleo and Charles Kindleberger. In their essays, they take their habitual attitudes. Kindleberger stands by his transatlantic experience, of someone who, as a young American, helped Europe back on its feet after World War II, by taking part in the grandiose experiment in American Aid called the Marshall Plan. Calleo plays his usual role of hard-headed real politiker, devoid of the romanticism of which he accuses Susan Strange. It is an attitude for which I have myself a lot of sympathy.

Calleo and Strange are, however, united by their seeing large companies and states as the main actors on the international scene. Strange believed that state power is on the wane, to be replaced by the largely incoherent power of large companies, both financial and industrial, whose exclusive strive for private profit is bringing world affairs to a state of semi-perpetual chaos. Calleo, on the contrary, is convinced that there are still a few national economies, run by alliances struck by states with their financial and industrial corporations. He sees two in particular being overwhelmingly relevant for world affairs in the next few decades, the US and China.

So, between Calleo and Strange, it is only a question of betting on who wins, but the horses in the race are the same, powerful states and powerful companies. And, in spite of her justified resentment against the US government, to which Kindleberger takes the strong objection of the honest American patriot, who lived his youth in the most farsighted age of US foreign economic policy, Strange seems still convinced of the possibility that a return to sanity by the US government might be able to bring back a measure of equilibrium in world affairs. Calleo underlines the fact that a reaffirmation of American hegemony in world economic affairs occurred in the 1990s, just as economists, political scientists and even anthropologists had finished explaining the profound reasons why the US had forever fallen behind Japan and the other East Asian tigers, and even Europe.

As I said at the start, I tend to share Calleo's faith in the persistence of a few important national economies, run by powerful interaction between the state and private enterprise. Like him, I believe that the Yalta system is still partly functioning. How could we otherwise explain the limited sovereignty under which the losers of World War II, the former Axis powers, still labour? The very special relationship which has taken shape since the war between Japan and the United States is indispensable to explain why Japan constantly heeded economic policy recommendations which came from the US Treasury and were almost always highly dangerous, even destructive, for her economy and polity. In the case of Germany, the US pushed the rest of Europe to agree to the formation of the European Common Market, to give Germany a market for her massive investment goods industry and thus re-establish her at the centre of Europe, a valid bastion against Soviet power. Again, it was Bush's father who organized the crucial negotiations which brought back a united Germany. And it has been the German government, together with the Italian, promptly to answer G.W. Bush's call to share the space shield development effort with the United States. The Italian government, moreover, has gone as far as contradicting previous decisions about the Kyoto agreements on climate control to please the United States administration.

I do not think Susan Strange would have found particular inspiration in the memorable quip, by one famous Speaker of the US House of Representatives, that 'all politics is local politics'. Neither seem to do Kindleberger and Calleo. Nor, *a fortiori*, does Geoffrey Underhill, if we have to judge by the sentence Strange quoted and I reproduced here.

This is my main objection to her outlook on world political economy. To my mind, foreign policy is but the continuation of the domestic political economy. It is true of all countries, but is doubly true of leading countries. In the case of a phase of world affairs when there is a clear hegemony, it is mandatory to study how local politics works inside the hegemon, because what is good for General Motors or for Microsoft is not only good for America but for the whole world. Or, to follow Calleo's lead in this book, how the dramatically increasing contrast between urban and rural China will be resolved matters for the whole world of the next few decades.

Susan Strange correctly pays great attention to the liberalization of American banking which began in 1980, with the Depositary Institutions Deregulation and Monetary Control Act. She sees it as the starting point of the degenerative spiral which induced the liberalization of the whole world financial system and the opening up of the Capitalist Casino, with central bankers rapidly transformed from controllers into croupiers and the inception and prevailing of *Mad Money* as the final stage. Neither she nor Calleo seem to be interested in knowing why it was in 1980 that the Financial Deregulation Act was passed, and what were the forces that led to its adoption by the US Congress.

Yet, it is not hard to reconstruct the historical process which saw one section of the American financial industry, the New York large commercial banks, patiently unravel the cloth of financial regulation throughout the last fifty years, in order to go back to the rank they had enjoyed before the Roosevelt financial reforms had declared them responsible for the Depression and condemned them to pay for it by a stunted existence as shadows of their proud former selves. How, by patient and constant effort of political influence those banks, after they achieved remarkable financial muscle through a spate of merger and acquisitions in the late 1950s, with the favour of the Republican presidency and Congressional power, gradually regained a larger and larger political and economic space in the 1960s and 1970s, is indispensable to understand why they scored such impressive victories in the 1980s and 1990s.

It helps, of course, to know that investment banks are, generally speaking, on friendly terms with the Democratic political establishment, while large commercial banks have a special relationship with an important section of the Republican Party. Walt Wriston, for instance, the legendary CEO of City Bank, perhaps the most important American, and therefore world, banker of the last fifty years, father of the most crucial financial innovation of the last decades, the Certificate of Deposit, was a declared Republican, an extremely influential adviser to Republican presidents.

But it is also necessary to go back to much earlier times, to understand why American banking developed as it did, with a core formed by very large commercial banks located mostly in New York and specializing in wholesale banking. This was a wholly American speciality, due to the very early prohibition, dating back to the National Banking Act of 1860, of branch banking, later confirmed by other legislative instruments, and gradually eroded in the post-war decades, till its very recent repeal.

The prohibition of branch banking is restricted to the United States. In other countries big commercial banks had their enemies, but they usually concentrated their efforts in fostering the establishment of a layer of deposit-taking institutions run on the principles of mutuality, rather than private profit maximization. They were called savings banks, people's banks, and the like. The political forces which were behind them were not strong enough to prevent the development of large banks' huge branch networks. This was the case everywhere, except in the United States, where a permanently strong coalition of debtors and local politicians managed to legally restrict large banks to the cities, by making branching illegal.

This led the commercial banks to specializing in inter-bank deposit-taking, collecting the deposits of small banks and placing them wholesale in the short-term money and financial markets. It was thus domestic politics and the laws it dictated which in the US induced markets, rather than large branch banking, to develop, and produced as the end result a financial system characterized by institutions unlike those of any other developed country. It was also the law which separated investment from commercial banking, and led the two sections to choose their political protectors. And laws are passed by Congress, the very place where all politics is local politics. It was very recently revealed that only a puny percentage of US congressmen have passports, a sufficiently dramatic revelation of their absolute preference for home haunts.

Historians will note that ours is the only time when a continent-sized nation has been the hegemon of world affairs. Rome, Austria, Spain, even England, were tiny compared to the empires they dominated. The US was still capable of generating 50 per cent of the increase in world trade in the five years leading to 2000. And it has attracted, in each of the last three years, more than 200 billion of foreign investments by far the largest share of the total the world has been able to generate in those years. The US private bond market dwarfs by its size any other private bond market. The same is true of Wall Street compared to other stock exchanges. Only in public bonds does the combined size of Euro markets prevail over the size of US Treasuries, and that is only because of the huge public debts piled up by Germany and Italy in the 1980s and early 1990s.

Since this asymmetrical structure has prevailed in the world economy in the second half of the twentieth century, and is, to my knowledge, an unicum in the history of international relations, it is imperative that foreign policy and international relations analysts become experts in the American domestic political economy. This applies even more strongly to international finance, where regulation and deregulation are as important as they are in the pharmaceutical, aviation and nuclear industry.

When Susan and I worked on the same project at Chatham House, back in the 1970s, we often discussed the possibility of studying how laws, regulations, standards adopted in the US for wholly domestic reasons soon get adopted by the whole world, in a silent but extremely powerful demonstration of real hegemony. People in other countries have awakened to realize that this had happened with English, which became the world language after the rise of the US to world power, and a great corpus of research has accumulated to study this phenomenon. Yet, in spite of our early realization of the general nature of this silent form of hegemony, we did not follow up on it, and there are so far only sparse and meagre publications that deal with it. Lawyers have noticed that the Common Law has prevailed in international commercial transactions, but are busy studying its vaunted superiority over Civil Law in regulating commerce. Our idea, back in 1970s, was that it did not matter whether an institution or a regulation was superior; the crucial element was that it existed in the largest domestic market in the world, which was rapidly getting connected to other domestic markets by imports. If you come from a relatively small country, and want to export to the US, it is indispensable to adopt the standards used in the US. After a while the penny drops, economies of scale do their work, and the exporting country finds itself adopting the US standard. There are, of course, exceptions. Electric voltage for home appliances is still set at 220 volts rather than 110 in most countries. But this is a question of choice of cost over danger in power transmission. Countries save a lot of money by using less copper for wires bringing electricity to homes. They pay a cost in the form of human lives lost by electrocution, but how many people are aware of this trade-off outside the world of electric engineers?

Another exception is the famous cellular phone standard unification, which occurred in Europe because of the determined action of governments, while in the US it was left to industry, and never occurred. As a result, cellular networks were united in Europe and highly segmented in the US, cellular phones boomed in Europe much earlier than in the US, and most world producers adopted the European standard.

This, however, is just an additional proof of the fact that when a highly developed and highly populated world region behaves like one nation, it can wield the same influence the only developed continental size country normally wields. An additional thought can be spared on Calleo's forecast about China's ascent in the not so distant future. Shall we all adopt Chinese standards? And in what fields?

Thus far, however, in the field Susan Strange chose to analyse most frequently and deeply, international money and finance, few would dispute that the US financial and monetary system, by its sheer size, has, for the best part of the last half-century, cast a giant shadow on the rest of the world. It is an objective way of projecting power, one which does not require any political decision from the top. Benign neglect, on which Kindleberger objects to Strange, is just an ex-post rationalization of a behaviour, rather than a policy. The Bretton Woods System remained in power as long as it did not interfere with US domestic policy-making. When it did, it stopped functioning. This happened long before August 1971. The US lost gold reserves for the whole of the 1950s and the 1960s. It only managed to compel the two former major Axis powers, Germany and Japan, to keep their reserves in dollars, thus showing that Yalta was still functioning.

Some well-informed analysts have even advanced the view that the end of Bretton Woods occurred because of a quarrel between the US Treasury and the Federal Reserve, exactly as the famous divorce between the same two agencies, back in the early 1950s, which had meant the end of Easy Money, had been a last revenge by a Marriner Eccles who knew he would not be reappointed and ordered the Fed to suddenly unload on the market a part of the Government Debt it held.

Robert Mundell, before and after his Nobel Prize, has written extremely well informed and revealing papers on world monetary history especially of the last fifty years. In his accounts, US domestic variables played an absolutely dominant role in determining the course of world monetary affairs since 1944. And, prominent among these variables, stands American economic theory, with its evolutions and convolutions. Personally, I tend to see theoretical developments as being the servants of politicians, who certainly want to be elected and re-elected, and have thus to read the minds of individual electors and powerful interest groups. Thus a theory suddenly comes into fashion, after having been neglected for years, sometimes whole decades, when it is useful to justify a turn in domestic policy dictated by much more mundane reasons. Monetarism and Rational Expectations are good examples. The first was good to justify the drive to deregulate US banking, as it maintained that it is not necessary to include banks in macro-economic control, as controlling the monetary aggregates more than suffices to keep inflation at bay. The second came very handy when Reagan was piling up public debt, as it proved that people know the model as well as the authorities and will not be fooled into believing that debt is a permanent substitute of taxation.

These two theories went back several centuries. Still, they came again into fashion when they were instrumental to US domestic policy-making, and from there, by the sheer displacement weight of the US political economy, they achieved rapid influence over the whole world.

The same had been true of Keynesianism. It became a world economic philosophy when the US adopted it as the theoretical background for the Marshall Plan and for much of its domestic policy-making. And it was displaced as a world economic philosophy and replaced by Monetarism and Rational Expectations when the US government decided to choose those two theoretical justifications for its domestic policies.

No conspiracy theory is however required to explain this hegemonic diffusion. It occurred because of the sheer relative size of the US monetary and financial system. It is perhaps worth adding that, in times of growing interconnection between world education systems, the sheer size of the US university system and its financial displacement power act as extremely powerful diffusors of US hard, social and human, sciences. Again, no top policy decisions are required. Demand for good brains is greater than supply in the US university system, where tough competition prevails, and salaries are freely negotiated. It thus attracts budding academics from the four corners of the world. These very intelligent people constitute a free and powerful mass of propagandists of US ideas and cultural practices in their own countries of origin.

In addition, the sheer number of US academics, plus their access to financial resources works powerfully towards the prevalence of US academic uses, standards, fashions, in scientific literature, which is not necessarily published in the US by American publishers but must adhere to what the largest market for scientific books and journals, the United States, dictates. In Economics, and I am told, in Sociology and Political Science as well, this hegemony of the US market has reached such extremes as to give place to a self-inflicted Americanization of research agendas and methods. Since most research consists in the replication and adaptation of the clever ideas and experiments of other people, research workers all over the world are busy conducting experiments, in the social sciences, on models dictated to US researchers by the US social and institutional context, and only thinly modified to answer contextual differences which other countries might present.

The huge relative size of the US market, in this age of fast communication and deep interconnection among markets, affects all facets of the international monetary and financial context. Apart from the prevalence of

US invented contractual forms and even names and fads in the financial context of other countries, it is appropriate to quote a method of institutional investments selection which has been adopted by the great majority of institutional investors anywhere in the world. It is the so-called world portfolio, where each national financial market must be represented by a value of shares or bonds which corresponds to the relative weight of the same market on world total. This means that Wall Street dictates over all other markets. No fund manager can ignore this method without risking his job. If in his portfolio the US market is underweight at the first relative underperformance of his portfolio he will be accused of rash speculation.

But there is much more than that. In options and derivatives, almost the entire US practice has been transferred to other financial markets through the international financial market. This means that, in case contractual problems arise, they will perforce have to be resolved by recourse to US legal methods. Again, because of the immense size of the US legal market, lawyers in the US have joined up forces in giant legal firms, which have come to dominate the world scene just by sheer size. Profitable and professionally rewarding niche positions and opportunities do of course exist for the enterprising little non-US firm, but the rules of the game are dictated by the big legal companies, again not because of their will to dominate but because they have a huge and impregnable home base over which they can defray fixed costs, thus being able to offer affordable legal services to non-US financial and industrial clients.

Again, a counter-example will help to prove the point. Because of the recent softening up of US courts on anti-trust cases, US companies, which have more than 500 million euros worth of business in Europe can bring other US companies to court before the European Commission's Directorate of Competition over alleged anti-trust violations, with the European Court of Justice functioning as Appellate Court. When an institution presides over the functioning of a continental sized market as big as that of the US, it immediately proves to be competition for the equivalent US institution, which had previously enjoyed a monopoly in the field.

How long will it take until this happens in more and more cases? Judging by the pace Europe is taking to unify its markets and institutions, it might just as long as David Calleo forecasts, in expressing his optimistic outlook on the future of US hegemony. He may be right, just by looking at defence, where Europe is progressing with leaden feet, and even at world climate control, where Europe is standing by the Kyoto Agreements and the US is reneging on them, dragging more and more countries with it.

But it is in the fields of money and finance where US hegemony is bound to last longer because of the displacement power afforded by the relative size of its domestic markets but also because of another feat of cultural hegemony, the Statute of the European Central Bank. This is a really bizarre case of involuntary imperialism. In the 1960s and especially in the 1970s, there raged in the United States a heated debate on central banks' independence, which was carried over in theoretical economics in the 1980s and early 1990s. The debate was the natural intellectual offspring of Chicago monetarism, as it was maintained that central bankers should be given the sole duty of controlling inflation, which was supposed to be an exclusively monetary phenomenon, fired by an excessive supply of money created by the central bank, with the commercial banks linked to central bank money by a stable and predictable multiplier. Central bankers should be free from the influence of election-seeking politicians and of power-wielding interest groups. Their independence from all other powers ought to be given constitutional status. While all these strong principles were being affirmed by a part of US politicians and soon afterwards theoretically proved by economists who also provided a wealth of real life tests to support their theories, mainly by comparing the inflation records of countries with the independence of their central bankers, the Federal Reserve was serenely sticking to its Statute of 1913, which says nothing about inflation control as a central bank's priority and focuses, instead on the need to stabilize the structurally fragile US financial system. More and more turbulence in the financial markets having naturally followed their progressive liberalization in the 1980s, this priority did not find anyone to seriously challenge it. The discretionary powers of the Fed were, on the contrary, regarded as extremely useful in fighting turbulence and allaying crises. Its role as lender of last resort was performed so often in the 1980s and 1990s that some people started calling the Fed the 'lender of first resort' and to muse on the moral hazard problems it posed to the US financial system.

Meanwhile, in Europe, politicians and central bankers were busy trying to launch European monetary unification, after the debacle suffered by the EMS in 1992– 93. The European Central Bank was rapidly created, and firm dates were set for the locking up of exchange rates and the introduction of the European currency, the 'euro'.

The 1990s being an age of large public deficits in some European countries, especially in the so-called Club Mediterrané, comprising Italy, Spain, Portugal and France, Northern participants in EMU were very worried about inventing a system which could be used by Mediterranean freeriders to use the parsimonious northerners' hard-earned resources for their public expenditure binges. The concept of a central bank, totally independent from government and the banking and financial worlds, and exclusively dedicated, by Statute, to fighting inflation, very strictly defined as an annual rise in the European consumer price level of more than 2 per cent, by strict control of the European money supply, defined as M3, which was supposed not to increase by more than 4.5 per cent, came in very handy, although it had been virtually ignored, after the initial enthusiasm, in the US.

The states which created the EMU scored a first in monetary history by collectively renouncing monetary sovereignty, one of the oldest and most important prerogatives of statehood. They renounced it absolutely, because the European Central Bank was, by its statute preventing it from financing governments, also deprived of monetary sovereignty. And, to make things even more definitive, they signed the Stability Pact, severely limiting member countries' freedom to accumulate budget deficits.

When the European Union finally reached a stage where it would have been able to imitate the United States in its ability to impose a monetary seignorage on the rest of the world, it formally refused to do so. And it seems that even the seignorage Germany had benefited from, by the widespread use of the Deutschmark in central and Eastern Europe is disappearing, as holders of Deutschmarks in those countries are busy exchanging them for dollars, as the day approaches when they will have to be redeemed for euro banknotes, for fear of becoming known to fiscal authorities.

If we want to interpret the contrasting behaviour of the US and Europe in monetary matters, it looks as if domestic borrowers' coalitions continue to prevail in the US, while lenders' coalitions dictate their will in Europe. This is made clear by a look at the asset-liability ratios of the private sector in Europe and the United States. As David Calleo notes in this volume, the US has gladly played, in the last few years, the role of private borrower and private consumer of last resort, while the opposite role has been played by the Europeans.

The final explanation of this difference may rest with the behaviour of demographic variables in the US and Europe. In the US birth rates have not fallen as dramatically as they have in European countries, especially in some of them like Germany, Italy, Spain. Moreover, while the US has continued to absorb huge numbers of immigrants in the last decade, potential immigration from eastern and southern Europe has generated alarm in countries which think of themselves as being culturally homogeneous and have a tradition of emigration rather than one of immigration, like the US.

Countries where old people already prevail and will prevail even more in the future are obsessed with saving for retirement purposes. Those who rail against the so-called spendthriftness engendered in people by opulent State pension schemes, ought to pause and consider that where such schemes are extremely weak, as in the US, people do not save, while where State pensions flourish, people save a lot, enough to finance the consumption and investment habits of US spendthrifts. I think Ron Dore's contribution to this volume is one of the most thoughtful pieces on the subject of alternative pension modes that I have read so far. The attack stupidly brought by European governments against state pensions, in stolid imitation of a so-called American model, has meant that people's savings have been burned in the financial casino so brilliantly described by Susan Strange.

It will be perhaps the collective reaction of millions of disillusioned and almost involuntary savers-investors in Europe which will induce the realization of what Calleo advances as a clever provocation, the closure of the casino. Had it been for the European Central Bank to decide, the casino would have already closed, with a memorable international financial crash engendered by its strictly deflationary policies. That things have not yet developed that way we owe to Alan Greenspan, who has himself tried to close the casino, but has seen his every attempt frustrated by the popular reaction, in the US, against any temporary slowing down of the financial merry-go-round. Every time he tried to stop the party by withdrawing the punch bowl, the growl from the populace (and from their elected representatives) was so fierce that he had to put it back immediately.

Local politics, indeed, once again. My guess is that financial fragility is so structured into the US political economy, now in the extreme but ever present since the very first years of the Republic, that deflation can prevail only if it is made inevitable by a coalition of extremely powerful forces, which very rarely work to reinforce one another, finally to overcome, at least for a while, the permanent coalition of borrowers on which the American political economy was born and, to this day, thrived, even if that has meant giving the rest of the world a powerful mixture of prosperity and depression.

REFERENCE

Underhill, G.R.D. (1997), 'Private markets and public responsibility in the global system: conflict and cooperation in transnational banking and securities regulations', in G.R.D. Underhill (ed.), *The New World Order in International Finance*, pp. 17– 49, Basingstoke: Macmillan.

Index